So You Have to Have a Portfolio

So You Have to Have a Portfolio

Second Edition

A Teacher's Guide to Preparation and Presentation

Robert L. Wyatt III ■ Sandra Looper

CORWIN PRESS
A Sage Publications Company
Thousand Oaks, California

For information:

Corwin Press, Inc.
A Sage Publications Company
2455 Teller Road
Thousand Oaks, California 91320
www.corwinpress.com

Sage Publications Ltd.
6 Bonhill Street
London EC2A 4PU
United Kingdom

Sage Publications India Pvt. Ltd.
B-42, Panchsheel Enclave
Post Box 4109
New Delhi 110 017 India

Printed in the United States of America

Library of Congress Cataloging-in-Publication Data

Wyatt, Robert Lee, 1940-

So you have to have a portfolio : a teacher's guide to preparation and presentation / by Robert L. Wyatt III and Sandra Looper.— 22nd ed.
    p. cm.
Includes bibliographical references (p.   ) and index.
ISBN 0-7619-3935-0 — ISBN 0-7619-3936-9 (pbk.)
    1. Portfolios in education—United States. 2. Employment portfolios—United States. 3. Teachers college students—Rating of—United States. I. Looper, Sandra. II. Title.
LB1728.W93 2004
370′.71′1—dc222
        2003021580

This book is printed on acid-free paper.

03   04   05   06   07   10   9   8   7   6   5   4   3   2   1

Acquisitions Editor:	Rachel Livsey
Editorial Assistant:	Phyllis Cappello
Production Editors:	Julia Parnell and Sanford Robinson
Copy Editor:	Diana Breti
Typesetter:	C&M Digitals (P) Ltd.
Indexer:	Rachel Rice
Cover Designer:	Michael Dubowe

Contents

Preface to the Second Edition

Why We Wrote This Book

Portfolios have become commonplace assessment tools in schools of education and, in fact, in all disciplines of higher education. The professional portfolio has become important as an alternative assessment as well as a required assessment for teachers who seek National Board Certification. The portfolio is also a tool for assessing the folios and program reviews of universities seeking national accreditation. Many states now require teacher education graduates to develop a professional portfolio to show their prospective employers. Oklahoma teacher education graduates, for instance, must address fifteen competencies mandated by the state legislature and enforced by a commission on higher education. By collecting artifacts and reflecting on how those artifacts prove proficiency in the various competencies, educators show the commission that they can meet the demands of the classroom. However, there are few guidelines to assist teachers and prospective teachers to develop and effectively use portfolios as assessment tools. Although we found several books on assessment within disciplinary domains, few of those texts crossed over to be useful in other areas of learning. More educators have begun to analyze the portfolio as a professional development tool, but most of them still approach the portfolio from a highly theoretical perspective. We found few publications that dealt with both the theory and technique of developing a portfolio and using it well. We decided a good practical guide was needed, so we set about to write one. Those who acquired the first edition of this book have told us that our plan worked, but they would like to see more activities, updated information regarding technological aspects of portfolio development, and inclusion of various national standards for portfolio development.

What Is New in This Edition?

While the first edition of this book had essential information about portfolios, with strong theoretical foundations and our CORP process (Collection,

Organization, Reflection, and Presentation), we found that there were other issues that needed to be addressed. There were many who needed more information about electronic portfolios and the role technology plays in portfolio development. Others sought information on very specialized educational portfolios for national certification, for tenure, or for promotion.

We added Chapter 9 to consider the various options for electronic portfolio development, examining advantages and disadvantages. We added Chapter 10 to look at the portfolio that is required for National Board Certification, with the idea that any specialized portfolio could be adapted to fit the format with minor adjustments. With these additions, the book will better meet the needs expressed by the portfolio users.

Many have remarked on the practicality of the ideas presented in our book. The portfolio remains a viable assessment tool to be used by administrators, mentors, future employers, or others who would evaluate teachers and students. The new material has met the needs of students in our undergraduate and graduate classes, as well as those outside the classroom. Our plan is a practical approach for putting together a creative, yet summative, documentation of professional qualifications.

The Purpose of the Book

The purpose of this book is to offer universities, colleges, school districts, professors, teachers, applicants for National Board Certification, and students a primer for a practical approach to portfolio preparation. The book may be used for individual professional development, in teacher assessment for tenure and advancement, and in teacher preparation courses. It may also easily be adapted by disciplinary fields to help those who have to present a portfolio to understand both the theory and good practices for individual fields of study. We have defined a portfolio, given the theoretical base for the various kinds of portfolios, and shown how to collect data for an appropriate portfolio presentation. This theoretical and explanatory material is contained in the first four chapters of the book. These chapters deal with the importance of creativity in the collection, organization, reflection, and presentation of the assessment portfolio, a process we call CORP. They offer several tools for each of the processes and compare the portfolio process approach with the other disciplinary processes.

In addition to portfolio theory, we have included forms, guidelines, protocols, sample rubrics, and other practical materials to make the portfolio a working document that shows student teacher growth and student teacher accomplishment. We have added some sample exercises that could be used with the text to supplement the assessment and professional development aspects of portfolios. The practical tools of the portfolio are contained in Chapters 5 through 8, where the practitioner will find samples, checklists, and other hands-on materials for completing the portfolio project. Chapter 9 discusses the pros and cons of electronic portfolios. It explains how to develop an electronic portfolio, and the hardware, software, and technological considerations of creating an online or CD-ROM portfolio. Many online resources and examples are included for the reader. Chapter 10 looks at the special portfolio requirements of the National Board for Professional Teaching Standards and how the CORP process of portfolio building fits those requirements.

Who Can Use This Book?

Educators who teach the portfolio process to students, and experienced and novice teachers and administrators compiling portfolios, will benefit from this book. We have been teaching the portfolio process at East Central University in Ada, Oklahoma for several years, and we searched long and hard to find a single, useful text for both the theory and the process. When we found none that we thought practical or useful enough, we decided to prepare one that could be used in our classes. The book incorporates many of the templates we have found useful in our teaching and assessment as well as templates that have been developed recently as a result of the portfolio boom.

We have seen that students approach portfolio development with fear and trepidation. Without a guide, they have difficulty understanding the meshing of theory and application. We now have exemplary portfolios assembled, and prospective employers have commented that the portfolios presented by our students have made our students more marketable. Their portfolios show how convinced they are about their competencies. We feel that we have taken the fear out of the portfolio approach to assessment because more and more, education demands more individualized, sophisticated, and complex methods of documenting learning. The professional portfolio exemplifies that kind of expertise.

The Portfolio Can Work for You

We certainly are not the originators of the portfolio in educational assessment, but we have both used portfolios extensively in our teaching at both the elementary and secondary levels prior to our experiences in teacher preparation. We have tested the portfolio as an assessment tool with students at all three levels, and in addition we have used the materials in workshops and presentations at state, regional, and national educational conferences. Our theories and tools have been examined by the conference participants, and they've commented positively on the CORP approach to building a portfolio. Reviewers also enjoy the suggested processes, which make portfolios come to life.

We hope that this book meets your needs as well as it has ours. Since we have used these materials for several years, we have selected the very best resources that have helped our students. Our acronym, CORP, will help users of the material to more easily understand the process application. The portfolio can be a tool to allow teachers at every level to prepare well-collected, suitably organized, appropriately reflected on, and well-presented (CORP) portfolios.

Brief Chapter Overviews

Chapter 1 deals with the definitions of a portfolio and details the thoughts behind the development of the portfolio as an assessment tool. The chapter answers the following questions: What is a portfolio? What are the important factors that guide portfolio preparation? What is the difference between a portfolio and a scrapbook? Why do I need a portfolio? This chapter also discusses authenticity, ownership, and creativity in the preparation of the portfolio.

Chapter 2 details the developmental portfolio and its background as a tool for reflections on individual growth. The questions answered by the chapter include: What constitutes a developmental portfolio? What makes this kind of portfolio useful? How is a developmental portfolio different from other kinds of portfolios? What kind of student would prepare a developmental portfolio?

Chapter 3 discusses the showcase portfolio, highlighting its uniqueness as a tool for success and self-esteem building. The salient points of this chapter answer the following questions: What constitutes a showcase portfolio and makes it unique? How does one select the "best" materials for use in the portfolio? When is a showcase portfolio more necessary than any other kind of portfolio?

Chapter 4 characterizes reflection as a heuristic device in self-examination. Reflection is the backbone of the portfolio. It helps one gain ownership of the plan and design of the portfolio. The chapter examines the following questions: How do I evaluate the artifacts that I have found for the portfolio? What does self-reflection do for the compiler and also for the portfolio audience? How do I make the reflections wholly mine and yet acceptable to the assessors?

Chapter 5 is about the planning and organizational stages of the portfolio. It answers questions about what one must include in a portfolio and how the completed portfolio will look. The chapter examines the following questions: What am I required to include in the portfolio? What do I want to include? How should the completed portfolio look so that it truly reflects me? The chapter also presents various methods of organizing ideas and artifacts that will help the student be understood by the evaluators.

Chapter 6 delineates the importance of the audience and how the portfolio will help its compiler get good grades or get a job. The chapter helps the reader understand the following questions: Who will be looking at this collection?

How can I tailor the portfolio to meet my needs? How will the portfolio address professional standards? How do I know which artifacts to include? The chapter discusses the materials that are useful for obtaining a promotion, for faculty review, or for a capstone for graduation. It also attends to self-assessment tools as a part of the reflective process.

Chapter 7 contains the nuts and bolts of putting the work together and getting it ready for presentation to your desired audience. It answers the following questions: How do I assemble various portfolio components? What electronic sources are available to help me? How can I create an electronic portfolio? The chapter contains charts, forms, plans, protocols, and rubrics that will aid the evaluator who assesses the portfolio and the compiler to complete the personalized self-awareness journey that concludes with the final copy of the portfolio.

Chapter 8 contains details of the presentation of the portfolio to its audience. It answers the following questions: How do I prepare for an oral presentation? What questions are frequently asked during presentations and interviews? How do I integrate my portfolio during a job interview? This chapter gives the portfolio owner insight and ideas for better presentation and communication.

Chapter 9 provides resources regarding planning strategies for electronic portfolios, including recommended hardware, software, and Web page designs. Checklists, rubrics, and many online resources, including actual online Webfolios, are included. Whether a preservice teacher or an experienced educator, new possibilities regarding technology and the role it plays in portfolio development are provided.

Chapter 10 tells how one who is compiling a portfolio for the National Board Certification can use the precepts of CORP in that process. It answers the following questions: How is the portfolio an integral part of the National Board Certification process? How do I establish parameters for this specialized portfolio? How does the portfolio complement the Core Propositions of the National Board for Professional Teaching Standards (NBPTS)? How do the subject area standards help plan the portfolio? What are the special challenges for collecting data for this kind of portfolio? How are the NBPTS presentation goals unique? How are simple "reflections" and NBPTS "written commentary" alike? What are the rubric questions to check this portfolio format?

Acknowledgments

We appreciate the patience and help of many who assisted in the writing of this book and in preparing this second edition. We want to thank our families—spouses, children, and grandchildren—but especially our spouses,

Louise Wyatt and Benny Looper, for their encouragement during the creative process. Unless one has been through the process of writing a book and then looking at it again for a second edition, there is no way of understanding how much time has to be sacrificed. Our loved ones have stood beside us well, and for this we offer them special thanks. Special thanks also are extended to Dr. Becky Compton and Kim Harris for reading some of the text and making suggestions.

We are thankful for the electronic highway that has carried messages through this year of writing. Although the Web and its technology ensnared us at times, it has illuminated and expedited the messages between Seattle and Ada. For reduced telephone bills we are grateful.

Our students deserve a nod of appreciation. For several years, even before we thought of writing this book, our students have been our captive "laboratory assistants" for developing and trying new ideas. They have worked willingly, only complaining occasionally about the work and forms, and have made us aware of changes needed in teaching strategies. Their feedback provided us with the impetus for continued professional growth. We owe them a debt of gratitude.

We do appreciate our colleagues for their confidence in our ability to complete this project. We appreciate the help of colleagues at East Central University in designing rubrics and various other forms for making the process of portfolio preparation better for us and more relevant to the needs of our students when they prepare portfolios as the capstone for their professional education course work.

Thanks also to those who pioneered the ideas and values of portfolio assessment. We have studied from, listened to, and read about so many of them, and we have adapted many of their ideas in crafting our own theories of portfolio development. We owe each of you a heartfelt thanks.

We need to add a special thanks to those at Corwin Press who have guided us through these two processes of creativity. We are especially grateful to Rachel Livsey and Phyllis Cappello for their work on this second edition. Their faith in the book and its usefulness is greatly appreciated. We appreciate those who do the book layouts, those who edit, and those who do the difficult tasks such as proofreading our material. We certainly appreciate the marketing division of Corwin for their continued support of our work in the catalogs they prepare. We appreciate their marketing strategies, which have kept our book visible to those who could benefit from it in their classes or for their own personal use. We appreciate those who have purchased the first edition, and we would hope that this second edition will become just as valuable for you in your quest to have the best tools for portfolio preparation.

Without this assistance, we might not have persevered. We hope the reader is pleased with the reflections and new information found within these pages. They are truly the compilation of ideas, inputs, and personal philosophies of many people. Our book is a work of love of and for teaching. Between the two of us, we have accumulated so many years of watching teaching grow. All of us, no matter how long we have worked in the field, know that teaching is dynamic and continues to grow. Pedagogy, at whatever level, must also continue to evolve and offer new insight to those of us who teach. Knowledge of subject matter, skills in presenting that knowledge, and a good disposition toward that knowledge is what keeps education so dynamic and so alive. Education means a continued chance to maintain freedom for those who would be free.

The contributions of the following reviewers are gratefully acknowledged:

Theresa Sullivan Stewart
Associate Professor
University of Illinois at Springfield
Springfield, IL

Orest Cap
Professor
Department of Curriculum, Teaching, and Learning
Faculty of Education
University of Manitoba
Winnipeg, Manitoba, Canada

Deborah A. Zeis
Teacher
Charlotte Public Schools
Charlotte, MI

Karen Coblentz
Principal
Dassel Elementary, Dassel-Cokato Schools
Dassel, MN

About the Authors

Robert L. (Bob) Wyatt III is Professor of Education at East Central University in Ada, Oklahoma, where he has taught for the past 13 years. He also taught education courses as a graduate instructor at the University of Oklahoma while completing his doctorate. He taught at the secondary level in Texas, New Mexico, and Oklahoma, and at the college level in New Mexico and Texas for 25 years prior to achieving his master's and doctorate degrees. He has led more than 150 workshops and seminars for staff development during the last 15 years. He has twice been named Teacher of Excellence at East Central, an honor that can only be awarded every four years and is usually nominated by students and elected by peer review. He was among the top five teachers contending for Oklahoma Teacher of the Year while teaching secondary school. He has participated in the Oklahoma Commission for Higher Education portfolio review committees for several colleges in Oklahoma as part of their preparation for NCATE reviews.

Wyatt is a language arts specialist with a Ph.D. in both the elementary and secondary levels of language arts. He has taught undergraduate courses in methods for language arts, social studies (both elementary and secondary), and natural science (elementary); Clinicals I, II, and III; strategies for effective teaching (elementary and secondary); Portfolios I, II, and III; children's literature; young adult literature; psychology of education; foundations of education; Composition I; and grammar. He teaches graduate courses in modern philosophies of education, contemporary issues of education, advanced language arts problems, techniques of research, and public relations for school administrators and librarians. Wyatt has two other books published: *The History of the Haverstock Tent Show: The Show With a Million Friends*, published in 1997 by Southern Illinois University Press, and *Making Your First Year a Success: The Secondary Teacher's Survival Guide*, coauthored by Dr. Elaine White and published by Corwin Press in 2002.

In addition to his teaching, Wyatt is a selling artist of watercolor and oil paintings. He also has three novels out for publisher review, is a former owner/editor of a weekly newspaper, and is the author/publisher of three books of local history and several journal articles in national, regional, and state journals. He is the president, a director, and an actor at Ada Community Theater, ACT II.

Sandra Looper is Adjunct Professor at North Seattle Community College in Seattle, Washington, in the Parent/Family Division. She currently teaches two online education classes: Special Topics for Parents of Young Children, and Violence and Children Through UniversalClass.com. She also provides independent consulting and speaking for various organizations and serves as an online expert for The School Page. She has been a presenter and speaker for more than 150 professional development programs, with special interests in the areas of positive school climate, parent involvement, attitude and motivation, team building, technology, effective teaching, and portfolio development. She began an independent consulting business, Teaching From the Heart, in 1992, and is a certified trainer for On the Way to Success With Early Prevention of School Failure as well as an instructor for Parenting With Love and Logic.

An educator for 31 years, Looper has a B.Sc. in elementary education and an M.A. in counseling. She is certified as an elementary teacher, principal, and counselor, and has taught graduate and undergraduate university classes in school administration, early childhood and parent education, and curriculum and portfolio development. She served as Associate Director of an innovative elementary education program called Teachers Educating and Motivating Students (TEAMS), in which public school mentors, university students, and faculty worked collaboratively to better prepare education students for the "real world" of teaching. She has presented numerous papers on the role of portfolios through the TEAMS Project, as well as on the importance of mentoring. She has written articles for *The Teacher Educator*, *Principal*, *Connections in Education*, *Baseball America*, *Learning PK-8*, and many local newsletter and online articles.

1

Defining Portfolios and Their Purposes

Dr. Evans and Dr. Bruce, both integral to the education department's professional education division, are responsible for ensuring that the education students at their university meet the mandate from the state's educational governing body concerning professional portfolios. Their professional education students must prepare and be ready to exhibit these portfolios so that the school can retain its accreditation.

"Exactly what is this 'professional portfolio'?" Dr. Bruce asked.

"Maybe it's some kind of collection of professional papers, such as resumes and letters of recommendation, or maybe it's just a collection of professional items. Isn't that what a portfolio is in most fields? I know that writing classes require their students to develop a portfolio, too. One of my students complained about having to keep up with everything that she had written in her English classes. Perhaps we can get information somewhere on what portfolios are," Dr. Evans replied.

"I know that this is not just a new fad in education because I have seen it in many journals these past few years. I just wonder what we will prove by requiring such a document. We have plenty to do now to get across the methods and pedagogies of education. We are required to do assessments of all that work already. This memo says that this is a part of our new state assessment plan for education," Dr. Bruce said.

Special buzzwords have been rampant in educational circles for the past few years. Terms such as "critical thinking," "authenticity," "hands-on," "student-centered," "reflection," and "qualitative assessment" have been right at the head of the list. But perhaps the most provocative among the buzzwords has been "portfolio." Ironically, a portfolio can easily cover critical thinking, authenticity, hands-on, student-centered, reflection, qualitative assessment, and more.

What Is a Portfolio?

An educational portfolio is a very personal collection of artifacts and reflections about one's accomplishments, learning, strengths, and best works. The collection is dynamic, ever-growing, and ever-changing. It shows a student's growth (developmental portfolio), best works (showcase portfolio), or total output (comprehensive portfolio). It is a tool for reflection on the items collected, and must be approached from the point of view of the compiler (the owner of the materials in the collection), or from the point of view of an assessor (one who looks at and evaluates that compilation of materials). The key concepts in portfolio revolve around collection, organization, reflection, and presentation (CORP).

The materials in a portfolio may be used by the compiler or the assessor as a ready reference, showing in an organized way just what the compiler has done. The portfolio offers an authentic framework for judging the effects of the work done by the compiler. It is a tool for evaluation by the compiler in self-reflection, or by a prospective or current supervisor. It serves as documentation that the compiler has reached a certain standard set for his or her professional area.

A portfolio is not a scrapbook, although it is something like a scrapbook in its presentational style. The selection of items for the portfolio requires some kind of reflection on why those items should be in the collection. If there is no reflection by the owner on the materials collected, the collection is merely a group of artifacts without form and purpose. It is the organization of the materials, with careful reflection on why the items in that collection were included, that make the collection a portfolio. Without the reflection, the material is just a folder or a scrapbook, and though each has its place in collecting and presenting relevant materials, the portfolio has the special capability of being viewed by an observer or an audience, who then can assess the value of the collection.

Some Background About Portfolios

The portfolio is not by any means a new phenomenon. Artists' portfolios, stock portfolios, and real estate portfolios have been around for many years, and they are similar to the portfolios that have recently been adopted in educational arenas as an alternative assessment, a qualitative method of assessing students' work. An educational portfolio has its own unique presentational style, but it is not unlike other kinds of portfolios.

An artist's portfolio is a collection of the artist's work. The artwork may be presented chronologically, showing the artist's progress from beginning work to current work. This type of presentation can be equated to the developmental educational portfolio.

Alternatively, should the artist choose, the work presented in a portfolio may be a showcase of the artist's best works. Often, the artist will arrange the pieces in the portfolio to show what he or she thinks is the ascending order of the best work done. Or, the artist could select only a very few of the works from a full career and then explain to the audience viewing the portfolio why each piece earned its particular place in the portfolio's order. Either of these arrangements would represent something like the showcase portfolio in educational parlance.

Finally, the artist could present everything created since starting in the art field. The items in such a portfolio could be in a logical order, or they could be chaotically stashed in the portfolio folder. This would be similar to the comprehensive educational portfolio.

The artist chooses pieces according to the audience and the purpose of the portfolio. Both help to determine how to present the artwork in the best possible light. The artist's audience may be a prospective buyer of the art pieces. Perhaps the audience is the owner of a gallery where the artist would like to display the artworks. The artist may be trying to impress an employer who is willing to pay for the artist's creative abilities. Whatever the audience or purpose, usually the artist compiles the items in some kind of presentation folder, but rarely does the artist include written reflections in the portfolio collection. Generally, the portfolio merely shows the artwork. Occasionally the artist may have to reflect in some way on his or her collection in an oral presentation, to justify the order or significance of the work so that it will be acceptable for display or ownership. This type of reflection is comparable to the reflection on artifacts in an educational portfolio. It may be a justification for the format of the entire portfolio or the inclusion of a specific item in the collection.

A stock portfolio also requires choices to be made by the compiler of the portfolio. This collection may be a comprehensive listing of all the stocks owned by the compiler, displayed to tell others what is owned. It may also be nothing more than a list of stocks, to show the owner's ability to select good stocks. The first example would be a comprehensive stock portfolio, and the second may be considered a showcase or a developmental portfolio for stocks. However, if the purpose of the portfolio is to explain the items selected to a first-time stock purchaser, the portfolio could require some very specific explanation, and require reflection on why a particular set of stocks were selected to work together as a business portfolio. These portfolios are similar to the educational portfolio, but the presentation may not be nearly as thorough, because the audience may not need the collector's reflections on which stocks are included in the portfolio.

The real estate portfolio is nothing more than a collection of real estate deeds, to show which pieces of property the owner has acquired. There may have been some reflection on the owner's part when certain purchases were made, to justify placing that material in a real estate portfolio. This kind of portfolio is akin to the comprehensive educational portfolio. The difference is that the real estate portfolio contains no written reflections on why the pieces of real estate are in the portfolio. The compiler, however, would certainly have some reflections when he tries to sell the properties he has listed in the portfolio.

What About Educational Portfolios?

Whatever the type of portfolio, the compiler must be aware of and be ready to explain why the collection was made and why it is presented in a particular way. The educational portfolio is not too different from the previously described portfolios. In education, portfolios have also become tools for assessment. Since teachers have to meet standards set by state mandates or accrediting agencies, they have to prepare portfolios as their avenue to meet those standards. The portfolio may be used as an assessment to move the compiler to a new level of education, or it may be used to promote the compiler. It also may be used to show the growth or potential growth of the compiler. Items in the collection must have some kind of value to the compiler and to the portfolio's audience. The compiler knows in advance who the audience is and has a clear-cut purpose in preparing the collection. He or she needs to justify the purpose of each artifact, stating why that artifact is included in the collection for the specific audience to whom the portfolio is addressed.

Historically, portfolios made their entry into education in the art field. Art portfolios in education were like the regular art portfolio in that they had no written reflections; they were merely collections of artifacts. Artists compiled their works in a large carrying case so that they could show their pieces to others or look at their own collected pieces. Later, for assessment purposes, art students who turned in their portfolios for grades had to be very selective about which pieces they included, and they also had to write or narrate some kind of reflection on the reason each of the specific pieces was included in their collections.

Then came educational portfolios in the English and language arts field. Writing teachers had long been experiencing a terrific inundation of paperwork to grade. Students had to prepare a great deal of writing to assure their writing teacher, their parents, and the school districts that they met the writing standards of an educated society—a society that was being goaded by rapidly expanding, sophisticated technological advancements. The writing portfolio was introduced and became a huge success, particularly with the overworked evaluator of the writing: the English teacher. Proponents of the writing portfolio system touted it as relieving teachers from having to read and mark carefully every paper their students wrote. These teachers began to see some light at the end of the overwhelming grading tunnel.

The writing teacher had, for several years before the development of the writing portfolio, organized peer writing groups in which members had input into each other's writing pieces. The writing process had already gained prominence in writing classes. This writing process generally consisted of a five-stage program for students to follow, in which they helped each other polish their work before the teacher saw the pieces for grading. This alleviated some of the reading and grading problems, but it did not really reduce the load. It just postponed the papers coming into the teacher's hands until the peer group had already done some evaluation and made suggestions for improvement.

Various writing specialists have their own ideas about what constitutes the writing process. Murray (1968) was among the earliest to say that writing was an identifiable process when his book, *A Writer Teaches Writing: A Practical Method of Teaching Composition*, introduced the idea of process. He discussed the following seven skills: discovering a subject, sensing an audience, searching for specifics, creating a design, writing, criticizing, and rewriting.

Later, in the 1980s, writing teachers generally agreed that all writers, whether professional or amateur, proceeded through five stages:

1. Prewriting (the stage in which the student collects and gathers material for a written paper on a chosen topic)

2. Drafting (a rough-draft document written after the student has collected sufficient data necessary for putting together the given piece)

3. Revising (a stage that requires the writer to examine the data and its first written presentation, changing anything that is erroneous or just does not sound good to the writer)

4. Editing (a stage after the writer has made desirable content changes that allows editorial corrections, such as spelling and sentence construction, to be made)

5. Sharing/publishing (the time when the writer of the piece is willing to allow others to read the written work)

Whatever the stages, English teachers were happy to see some pattern evolve because that allowed them to set up a system for assessing the written work by having a peer writing group help with the revising and editing stages. When written pieces came to the teacher for evaluation, they had already undergone some group evaluation, and the peer writers had suggested changes that otherwise would have required many hours of teacher observations. Peer writing groups made the process move smoothly by having students help each other correct writing errors involving both logic and mechanics. Writing improved. Apparently, English teachers were doing something right by having students work together.

But that still did not lighten the writing teachers' grading load enough. They needed further help because society still said that American students were not improving enough to meet the required standards. In the late 1980s, writing portfolios grabbed the attention of writing teachers. This program allowed students to take some responsibility for their own writing pieces by having each student select which pieces the teacher would evaluate. The writing students generally either selected a showcase approach, to show their best works over a given period of time, or they chose a developmental approach, to show their improvement in writing over a given period. Whichever approach the students chose, teachers were thankful for no longer having to read and grade every piece of their students' writing.

In either the showcase or development approach, once students gathered the materials, teachers could do a heuristic or holistic qualitative assessment of those items that the students had selected from their total works. Then, as a further device that allowed the teacher to confirm that the student knew why he or she selected the works presented for evaluation, they began requiring students to reflect on why they had chosen a limited number of pieces out of a large repertory of written work.

In cases where developmental ideals were sought, a student could explain how the selected piece showed growth in skills. This could be done by presenting a progression of materials, and describing why the items chosen showed development and writing progress. Or, the student showcasing written work could offer justification for the selection of showcase pieces for the portfolio.

This assessment technique quickly caught on and proved to be substantially better for the English teacher, easing the grading load tremendously by not requiring teacher examination of students' total writing output. The student writers felt authentic ownership of their own works, whether in a developmental or a showcase approach; they received some input from trusted peers in the peer writing groups, and perhaps let parents in on the final selection process. Even if the teacher (or the school district) required a comprehensive portfolio, the students could be asked to earmark particular pieces to be evaluated by the teacher, and they would still feel ownership of the material.

At present, the assessment portfolio dominates all levels of English education, from early elementary school through higher education. The English student and teacher are much happier with this authentic approach to assessment. Teachers feel that there is a greater sense of purpose in allowing students to choose those pieces with which they are most secure, or of which they are most proud. This pride of ownership seems to have made for better scores on standardized writing tests. Teachers are more satisfied now that their grading loads have been lightened.

Because the English departments of schools have seen the potential of the portfolio, other disciplines have picked up on the process. The portfolio has become a much-praised system of assessment in most educational disciplines. Science has lab portfolios. Mathematics has designed a portfolio approach to math projects. Music students can record their performances on audiotape, to show their development or showcase their presentational skills. Technology allows students to create interactive multimedia electronic portfolios.

In more recent years, colleges have adopted the portfolio as an alternative method of assessment. Many colleges now require that a general education portfolio be submitted as an exit requirement, prior to focusing on a specific discipline. Most of the disciplines, spurred on by assessment research or by the actions of various educational governing boards, also require some kind of portfolio. In some states (Oklahoma, for example), students seeking certification in teaching, at all levels and in all disciplines, are required to present a portfolio to complete their education degree. In many colleges, portfolios are required at both the undergraduate and graduate levels. Furthermore, some districts require a portfolio for promotional and tenure purposes. Portfolios offer an organized approach to showing student output, and they offer some proof that work has been done in given environments.

In some cases, school districts ask that candidates bring in a portfolio so that administrators and personnel directors may assess their work before they are interviewed. These employment portfolios are usually of the showcase type (because some border on scrapbook presentations, especially those that are commercially presented in a scrapbook format). But however the document looks, the point is that now the teacher (or teacher prospect) as well as the student must build a portfolio for assessment purposes, and the common education teacher must prepare one for job retention, promotion, or tenure. Even in higher education, professors have to present a portfolio in order to be promoted or to gain tenure in most colleges and universities.

The portfolio process is dynamic; that is, it is ever-growing and ongoing. The key to the process is not creativity, although creativity plays an important role in putting together a more palatable presentation. The real factor for assessment is the reflection. Reflection is a superior tool for presenting individuals and their work most effectively.

Is There a Process Approach to Portfolios?

The writing teacher spends time teaching the writing process. Though the stages of development vary, improved writing results from application of the process. Each writing teacher adapts the process to his or her own philosophy of teaching. As long as the teacher and the student realize that the process is not linear but recursive, it will work. Linearity simply means that one step logically follows another, and the second step cannot be taken until the first step is complete. In this instance, recursive means that from any stage in the process, the writer can jump back to a previous step or move forward to any step in the process as progress is made toward the presentation stage. Most creative work is by nature recursive and does not have a specific hierarchy for development.

We have developed a process approach to portfolios that should help the teacher and the student to understand the items that must be present for the portfolio to be complete, effective, and successful. The acronym CORP describes our approach to portfolios, our process approach. The letters in CORP represent the following operations in the portfolio process: *collection* of data, *organization* of data, *reflection* on the selected data, and *presentation* of the product. Just as in the writing process, the portfolio process is recursive. At any stage in the development up to the presentation stage, the data may be changed, rethought, and adjusted. These changes are what makes the portfolio dynamic rather than static. A scrapbook, on the other hand, is static. The photographs and items in a scrapbook would likely all be chosen for the scrapbook for a specific purpose, and though they could be altered to change the mode of presentation without reflection, they are virtually unchanging and sit still, without growth.

When students work on portfolios, however, they know that the material can and should be changed with the growth and reflection of the owner of the material. This approach does not, of course, mean that the compiler of a portfolio with a specific purpose and audience in mind can chaotically jump around with the data. The very idea of a portfolio suggests an organized presentation of the compiler's works, thoughts, plans, and so forth. The document must be made with a clear-cut purpose and a definite audience in mind, just as is required in a writing portfolio. Some universities have ignored these facts in setting very rigid, prescriptive guidelines in portfolio development. One can still have organization without the direct linear approach that says, "I must include this, then I must do this, then I must show this." A portfolio cannot be prescribed that meticulously, or the compiler loses ownership, and the purpose of the presentation is not clear to the compiler or the observer. One can choose any number of data, then limit the number from that expansive list, as long as each piece chosen has a reflection to make it an authentic part of assessment. Or, the compiler may throw out all of the many pieces of data previously chosen and gather an altogether new set of data for the presentation, making new reflections on the choices. One may repeat that process several times in the first stage of CORP, the collection stage. The portfolio can progress in that changeable manner all the way to the presentation stage, but the compiler might think of something else that should have been included to make the portfolio closer to completion. A recursive act can occur. The compiler can jump back and begin collecting new data even at that stage in the process. There is no need for linearity when one may recursively look again at the document and make changes at any stage of the CORP process. On the other hand, the compiler may have a plan so well mapped out that the process approaches linearity (some people are that meticulous in their own organizational techniques and can set their own prescriptions), but he or she will still use a great deal of creativity to present the items, so that their inclusion is justifiable to the audience and to the purpose of the specific portfolio.

What About Creativity?

Creativity is a very important part of any educational or life-enhancing pursuit. Creativity is definitely a part of portfolio preparation and presentation, regardless of the portfolio's purpose or its compiler's teaching discipline. In order to appropriately train a student in the creative processes, one should be aware of the stages of creativity. Goleman, Kaufman, and Ray (1992) list the five stages of creativity as preparation, frustration, incubation, illumination, and translation. Their approach to creativity is expanded linearity, also. The last stage must have all the other preceding stages in it, but otherwise the stages are somewhat flexible. Once the creative being experiences the illumination stage—the "Eureka!" moment, when the light comes on in the darkness—there is less recursiveness because a definite end is in sight, but the illumination may cause one to become totally recursive to clarify his or her idea. Goleman et al. further state that the "act of creation is a long series of acts, with multiple and cascading preparations, frustrations, incubations, illuminations, and translations into action" (p. 23).

Every person has certain thought processes that involve creativity. Gardner (1993) divides the various thought processes into nine categories that he refers to as "multiple intelligences." He has spent a great deal of time in written discussions and documentations of these various intelligences, and he ties creativity into each of them. He certainly advocates the importance of creativity as other authors have delineated it, but he himself has also written a book on creativity and the development of creative processes. Gardner suggests that one can work in his or her own way to build a creative piece, and that when each works at an individual speed and thought process, though there is variety in the created pieces, there is a final creative piece that has some appeal across the thought patterns.

I may have one idea for the organization of my portfolio, and I may approach that idea with very creative, artistic artifacts because I am a writer and a visual artist. That would not mean that mathematically or scientifically oriented persons could not have the same quality of portfolio, using that which appeals to them in pulling together their ideas for presentation. The difference would be, perhaps, in the portfolio's appearance, not in the kind of material presented. The way one sees and reflects on the artifacts would constitute the main difference in the portfolio's appearance. The artist would, perhaps, have an artistic flare in the artifactual presentation; the mathematician would, on the other hand, have a more logical approach in presenting the materials and reflecting on them. Both approaches would be acceptable, with neither presenter being right nor wrong. As long as a plan and the basic CORP approach is followed, the compiler is right because that compiler has to decide which artifacts best support the premise that the portfolio is trying to articulate.

Because the portfolio is now required in many educational settings, some teachers or schools are making the portfolio, and what is to appear in it, very prescriptive and somewhat mechanical. For instance, some state that all portfolios must be presented in a specific folder or binder. Some are giving the students a list of artifacts that must be included in the portfolio (transcript, letters of recommendation, videotapes, CD-ROMs, etc.; see Resource F). There would appear to be little creativity in this type of mandatory format and material, but the fact is that the creativity is in the student's reflection on the reason a specific piece of documentation is included.

Questions occur to the compiler during reflection: Why did I choose the specific artifacts I have finally decided on for the portfolio? How does the artifact substantiate what I am setting out to prove or support? Where does this piece fit into the overall picture I am trying to present? Will my audience understand my choice of an artifact and my reflection on it? All of these questions are pertinent and all should be answered, but once the compiler is satisfied that the material is correctly done and adequately represents him or her, the portfolio becomes a documentary as well as a personal assessment tool.

Looking at the Portfolio as an Assessment Tool

Once the portfolio is agreed upon as an assessment device, those involved with the portfolio need to reach agreement as to what should be examined for the presentation. They need to decide whether the portfolio will be seen by peers, a teacher, a committee, or by a supervisor—in other words, who the audience will be. The audience is perhaps the single most important factor in setting up the prescription for a portfolio. When a teacher sees that a student needs to improve in a discipline, perhaps the best kind of portfolio would be a developmental portfolio. The teacher and the student would have a portfolio conference to determine the kinds of materials that would be of greatest benefit for evaluation. Though they would not select pieces together to use as artifacts in a specific portfolio, they would discuss the kinds of items that perhaps could be used in the portfolio. The preparer still feels ownership, yet the observer/ assessor also has a responsibility in the process.

The co-working approach leads the compiler to know what the assessor would like to see in a portfolio, and also helps the compiler understand the process of evaluation and thus engage in self-evaluation. The reflection part of portfolio preparation is really nothing more than a written self-evaluation. Students evaluate artifacts they want in their individual portfolios based on what the teacher has articulated for the assignment. The student still maintains authority and ownership over the work presented, but knows more or less what is expected from the portfolio conference.

The portfolio conference may be worked through in a simulation in peer groups, so that students may discuss among themselves what they think their instructors want. However, one of the important factors in portfolio preparation is that each of the students may be preparing a different kind of portfolio based on that individual's specific needs. That is one of the important factors in using portfolio assessment. Some students need to show progress, whereas others need to showcase best works. The portfolio is a very individualistic assessment tool that would be similar to a special education teacher's writing an Individualized Education Program (IEP) for each student in the special education classroom. That is one of most important factors in individualized assessments. Each student is evaluated based on that student's individual need. A teacher who uses that tool will find the successes and self-esteem building from making each portfolio an important project. This will indirectly cause the student to make more rapid progress toward an individualized goal.

The Role of Goal Setting in the Portfolio Process

Once students know that they will be evaluated on the artifacts and their reflections on each individual artifact, they will begin to realize that in order to reflect on a piece for presentation, they must have a goal in mind. If a teacher can point out the value of goal setting before the artifacts are accumulated, the students will more effectively search for or prepare their artifacts for their portfolios. They must be instructed as to the purpose that a piece is to achieve, whether the piece is a found piece of documentation for a specific competency, or whether it is a document or problem that the students themselves prepare. They must be aware of the "why" of an assignment. What teacher has not been asked, "Why do I have to do this assignment?" Using the portfolio approach will also help teachers assess the value of their assignments, because they will need to know themselves why they assign a specific project, research paper, article, problem, physical activity, and so forth. The teacher's introspection about student assignments becomes valuable to both parties. Reflections make for better students. They also make for better teachers who are more aware of students' needs while they are collecting data for the first stage of the portfolio process.

Another important factor is that this approach to collecting data can be used for students at every capability or maturity level. The process and the assessment cause different goals to be set for each student preparing a portfolio. This has been effectively demonstrated at the secondary special education level, where students become exuberant in their collections and selections of the proper materials to substantiate their reaching specific goals that they, with the teacher's and parents' help, have set. They can feel the same satisfaction in their presentations as those at the upward end of the capability stage. That is why the process is valuable for all to know and use.

It is beneficial to engage in assessment regularly. Once a goal has been set, gathering data to help show that the goal has been achieved becomes important. But when one reflects on an artifact for substantiation of achieving that goal, then the reflection is the most creative and important part of the assessment, not the collection of the artifact. However, one has to have a goal and an audience in mind when the process begins. If you know your audience and your goal, you will not stumble around in trying to achieve it.

Planning a trip is analogous to reaching goals in the portfolio process, and the analogy is one that can be effectively used in planning and presenting a portfolio conference. When planning a trip to a distant city, for instance, the traveler has to know the purpose of the trip and the amount of money and time that is available for the trip. If I were going to travel to New York City from Oklahoma City so that I could see three specific Broadway plays, and I knew that I had only two evenings and one matinee time set aside to see these three shows, I would not plan to go to New York City via the leisurely route in an automobile. I would likely travel the most direct route. I also would set aside a specific amount of money for the tickets, lodging, and meals for the limited amount of time I would be in the city, and I would decide what I would wear and how I would move from place to place within the city. I also might have to justify to myself (reflect on) why I chose to do the trip in such a short time, how I would spend my money, and where I would stay to be near the various theaters showing the plays. I would set goals (making the trip with its special limitations), reflect on those goals, and accomplish them for a presentation to my friends upon my return. This kind of goal-setting activity is similar to what needs to be done in the preparation of a portfolio.

Summary

A portfolio is an evaluative tool (whose parameters are decided on in advance) for presenting a person's developmental growth works, best works, or comprehensive works. The artifacts presented in a scrapbook fashion are each reflected on in written or verbal documentation, showing how the compiler has reached a specific goal with the presentation of the portfolio. Portfolios concentrate a student's work, giving the teacher or evaluator a chance to focus on what the student wants that evaluator to see.

Questions

1. What is the CORP plan and how does one use it in portfolio preparation?
2. How does the writing process enter into this preparation?
3. What are the steps to creativity and what are their roles in portfolio making?
4. How would one differentiate between developmental, showcase, and comprehensive portfolios?

Topics for Consideration

1. Find two artifacts from a collection of data that demonstrate the competency that states "a teacher uses the best methods of motivating students to learn to think critically."
2. Write a reflection justifying each of the artifacts in a portfolio collection of the three types of portfolios.
3. Have a cooperative peer discussion concerning your perceptions at this point of the differences between various artifacts, to decide where they would fit in the developmental, the showcase, and the comprehensive portfolios.
4. Discuss the value of recursiveness in planning, as compared to linearity and prescriptiveness.

2

Developmental Portfolios
Documenting Personal Growth

Toshina Lambert has several students with different levels of ability in her classroom. She wants to show that her students are making progress and she has adopted the showcase portfolio as her method. She wants each student to feel comfortable with the portfolio process, but she recognizes that the showcase portfolio is not the answer for all students. Her dilemma is that she only knows about the showcase portfolio, but she does not think it is working well for Celeste and Sean whose educational plans are limited by IEPs. Celeste cannot spell, and Sean is a poor reader. Neither of them can "shine" with a showcase portfolio. Ms. Lambert approaches her supervisor with her dilemma.

"Why don't you try the developmental portfolio?" her supervisor asks. "In that way you can allow each student, including Celeste and Sean, to do the kind of portfolio that meets each individual's needs. Some students should do a 'best works' showcase portfolio. Others should show progress in the work they have done. The progress-enhancing portfolio is called the developmental portfolio, which shows how a student has grown from the first lesson up until the present. I suspect that the developmental portfolio will be the best fit for Celeste and Sean, and they will still be doing an individual portfolio."

What Is a Developmental Portfolio?

A developmental portfolio is one that shows the growth and development of students as they progress from one learning stage to another. The developmental portfolio is, as are all other portfolios, designed to be an individual's case study, but instead of showcasing best works, it is the study of one's growth and development during a given period of time. This kind of portfolio is still not a scrapbook in which there is no analysis and no definitive plan in mind, with every artifact chaotically arranged in a binder or folder. Instead, it shows a progression of development, moving from Point A upward toward Point B. The person preparing the portfolio reflects on each artifact, placing the artifacts in order to show growth or maintenance of progress.

The developmental portfolio goes beyond the idea of showing "Who am I?" It takes the personality of the compiler and shows how that person develops through various phases of learning: "Who am I becoming?" This kind of portfolio is perhaps more difficult than the comprehensive portfolio because students must look at their total output, show some logical, sequential development, and then defend their logic in choosing that developmental order. It becomes cathartic for students because they have to look closely for benchmarks to determine how they have grown and what routes their growth has taken. These portfolios are not quite as recursive as other types because they must be organized hierarchically to show what the students have learned and accomplished. Of course, recursiveness is a part of choosing the hierarchy of the items, and compilers may go back and forth over which items should be chosen. So there is something recursive in the process of making their reflections define and show growth, but the recursiveness is not as evident as when one literally goes back and forth among the stages of the process. There is a definite linearity in just ordering items into a historical hierarchy. The question that each student must answer about the artifacts and reflections in this type of portfolio is "How does this piece show how I have grown in comparison with the earlier pieces that I have collected?" This type of portfolio is very reflective and retrospective in its nature.

What Is the Effect of the Developmental Portfolio?

One of the most interesting factors concerning the developmental portfolio is that if students see growth for themselves, they can take a great deal of pride in the ownership of their work. They have given their assessor evidence to prove that they have grown, and reinforced in their own minds what they have accomplished. If they have that reinforcement and have shown growth, then self-esteem builds and even the most developmentally slow student can show movement by showing improvement from piece to piece. In a developmental portfolio, the students demonstrate to their assessor that "I am making progress. I have proven that process by giving you the pattern of my progress."

The developmental portfolio may show just the tiniest bit of growth, but knowing that even *some* growth has occurred is very supportive and comforting to the student. When the observer, especially a teacher, can see the growth, there is also a feeling of accomplishment on the observer's part for having had a hand in the process of development. Again, growth generates growth from the perspective of the compiler or the assessor of the developmental portfolio.

In a developmental portfolio, one student may be able to show strides of growth whereas another shows just faint glimmers, but there is a special built-in pride in seeing whatever amount of advancement that has occurred. Movement is the prerequisite for the developmental portfolio. This kind of portfolio is dynamic because there is movement, and a portfolio of any kind is designed to teach the compiler that life is not static. So a developmental portfolio would be assessed favorably if any growth at all is shown and justified by the owner's reflections.

In a special education class, the developmental portfolio can be an extremely valuable assessment tool. Reflections may be presented differently in these portfolios. Students who may not have writing capabilities, for instance, may reflect on their presented artifacts orally. This may be nothing more than just showing their joy at being able to choose their own artifacts to indicate that they are moving upward in their educational life. Some states are now requiring alternative assessment portfolios by the special education students, and even those who are severely or profoundly disabled must participate by having developmental portfolios done for them.

What Questions Might Be Asked?

In all portfolios, the compiler or student must have ownership of the work. Students' portfolios must reflect that ownership, and teachers can ensure this by allowing students to choose artifacts that they feel show their style of ownership. Developmental portfolios need to be organized in the same way as any other portfolio.

As the compiler collects data (C of CORP) for a developmental portfolio, a primary question is, "What did I learn during the time period this portfolio covers?" Students need to show their audience the struggle they had to select the artifacts that demonstrate their growth. They have to choose information that would help them reflect on their struggles, and they have to ask themselves, "What did I learn?"

In a very advanced class on how to build a portfolio, students were asked to show their developmental growth. Though all of the students were in the classroom during the portfolio presentation, each student reflected on a new or different concept learned from the presentation. Their list was almost startling because each of them learned something different. The presenter listed a set of objectives for the participants, and the students developed in their own ways. They learned the objectives set by the presenter, but each gained the knowledge from a different perspective. Each had a different grasp, a different development. With their own unique answers to "What did I learn?" each had the makings of a good developmental portfolio. Individual growth is the most important factor in developmental collections and reflections.

How Does One Set Up Parameters for Collecting?

Because students are the owners of the material presented in the portfolios, they must be a part of the organizational planning (the O of CORP), and must be involved in choosing what kinds of documentation need to be in the portfolio. They also must be involved in establishing an evaluation protocol (rubric) for scoring or evaluating the portfolio. If they have ownership of both the portfolio and the rubric, they will be much more adept at showing how they have met the rubric's requirements.

Consequently, one of the first things that should be done is to set up a group discussion. Most of the group members should be peers, but the teacher/ evaluator should be part of initial groups. As a group, they must set criteria for the kinds of items to be included in their portfolios. If the teacher is not a part of the initial planning group, the group should make a presentation of its plans so that the teacher can have input into the criteria. If the portfolio is to be owned by the students, they must be a part of rubric creation.

After parameters have been set, checklists should be made available so that the checking process is easy and thorough. The checklist is usually devised by the teacher after students have verbalized what they think should be covered in the assessment. Some institutions may be confined to state mandates or university-generated protocols in which the student has little input. Regardless, the checklist allows students to have a continuous appraisal of where they are in the portfolio-building process. They can keep the checklist in hand as they prepare their presentational portfolio, and the teacher can certainly use a portfolio checklist to substantiate ongoing preparation and growth.

Portfolio making is a holistic process for students because it involves the whole of their beings. Even something as simple as the students' getting up before their classes to discuss their portfolios helps the students to become better developed. This gives all the participants a chance to have a sense that they belong to a group. Speaking before a group, or making audiotapes of presentations made throughout a semester, could also make excellent artifacts for the presenters' portfolios. The possibilities for showing growth are limited only by a student's creative imagination. As we've noted previously, the keys to success with a portfolio are documentation and reflection. The basic premise is to give credence to one's achievements by showing "What and how I have learned."

McLaughlin and Vogt (1996) indirectly describe the developmental portfolio when they discuss schema-based learning development. They note that "learning takes place when new information is added to previously acquired knowledge" (p. 10). The developmental portfolio is the product that proves that learning has occurred. Teachers greatly influence what is learned by aiding the students who otherwise cannot make the connections about how much advancement has occurred in their learning. Fundamentally, the answer to the question "What have I learned?" lies with the student, and part of that learning is the capacity to show what has been learned with artifacts and reflection.

The Learning Process That Results in Good Assessment

When assessment takes place, there are certain perspectives that have to be understood. When students realize the possibilities for assessment there is growth, and when there is growth that stems from some mild inquisitiveness or curiosity, there seems to be learning. Narrowing the concepts into something that can be measured can cause a great amount of difficulty for the portfolio compiler and the assessor. An integrative approach to learning seems to require five stages of activity on the part of the learners. That process is still changing, but at present it appears that the five stages for acquisition and retention of knowledge are investigation, discussion, demonstration, writing, and construction. All the activities should be performed by the student, not the teacher. If students accomplish these stages on their own, there is no logical reason they will not be able to perform adequately when asked to showcase their knowledge.

The Five Stages of Learning

The investigation stage is the time for the learner to gather data. It is very similar to the collection stage of CORP in portfolio design. If the learners gather their own data and understand what they gather as they gather it, then the material collected by them will have a higher chance of being retained. Investigation includes such things as listening to teacher lectures, looking at resources in the library, reading textual material, and engaging in any other kind of activity for gleaning information and fortifying the mind of the student who is doing the investigation.

Discussion takes a different turn in this kind of student-oriented work. Discussion has often been characterized by the teacher asking questions and the students responding. In this context, however, the students would discuss in peer groups whatever information they have collected. Working together as peers in discussions of learning is the solidifying activity for the developmental portfolio. Generally, once a topic is announced by the teacher, peer groups are instantly formed or existing peer groups respond to the teacher's announcement of the subject. In portfolio peer groups, the group may move directly to the discussion of their investigations and possible items for portfolio inclusion. Indeed, if the portfolio group has five members, and if each student in the group shares information on collected artifacts, then there is really five times the amount of learning occurring. Furthermore, the student's verbalization of the material considered for inclusion in the developmental portfolio aids in retention.

The third activity slated for the peer group is a demonstration, in some fashion, of the material that the peer group has decided is relevant to understanding the competency or learning objective. Each member of the peer study groups will participate in some kind of demonstration of the material that the group deems relevant for the portfolio presentation. This presentation is a physical demonstration of what they feel is important. If the competency requires that they understand multicultural education, then the group may document such learning with a folk song they have recorded from another culture for inclusion as an artifact in their portfolio. They also may demonstrate their learning by showing photographs of the historical buildings in the town as part of a unit on local history in a lesson plan that they have taught in a clinical setting. Each person in a peer group should have a chance to validate the artifacts within the group. Surely the quality of the developmental portfolio will be higher because group members have now investigated, discussed, and demonstrated a thorough understanding of the artifacts they have chosen. Even more important, all have had their learning reinforced by hearing several peers justify their collection of artifacts. The teacher may have to fill in some relevant details, but the teacher's load has been minimized, and the students' learning has been maximized. Though they realize that their teacher knows more, the material that students learn is often more palatable when it comes through the mouths of their peers, in their own language.

The fourth step in this learning process is the compositional or writing stage—the reflection. Remembering that these listed learning activities are not hierarchical, the students may opt to do the writing before they actually get up and demonstrate their learning. The point is that they have a fourth opportunity to show how much they know about the chosen artifacts, and if they share their writing with their peer group or the entire class, they are getting a great deal more exposure to the subject. Certainly, such extra exposure will enhance their developmental capabilities.

After investigation, discussion, demonstration, and writing comes the final stage: construction. This is the tactile and visual stage for the learner. Construction requires that the portfolio compiler understand the process of the portfolio organization. Each student must know that he or she can construct something that shows his or her development through various stages.

These five stages of learning go hand in hand with McLaughlin and Vogt's (1996) list of five possible ways that teacher learning may occur:

> (1) learning about the innovative perspective, (2) choosing ideas that work in our context, (3) holding discussion with peers and administrators, (4) interacting with students to ensure the assessment system would be collaborative in nature, and (5) aligning the innovations with university grading policies. (p. 11)

The first two items listed above are closely related to the investigative process in the five-stage learning program we propose. The third point is compatible with the peer group discussion and demonstration of ideas. The fourth may be equated with the writing stage previously discussed. The final step they list is equivalent to the construction of projects. Either set of learning devices will work well for anyone who is trying to get at real retentive thought accumulation. The first four stages represent the stages of CORP process, with the actual building of the portfolio as the construction phase of the five-part plan for learning.

The basic premise is that there must be a plan so that an assessment or an evaluation of each student may be conducted. The portfolio compiler must have a part in that process so that understanding and awareness of the usefulness of learning occurs on a regular basis.

Reflections Are Necessary in Developmental Portfolios

Important questions concerning the developmental portfolio might include: "What does the portfolio show that I have learned?" and "Has my progress been adequate or must I concentrate on certain elements more fully to show my learning?" Keep in mind that the more open-ended an assignment is, the more difficult the assessment will be. Once the students get the concept of portfolios, then the task of constructing one will be a minimal process for them to accomplish. Once one has a process in mind, the task does not seem nearly so formidable. Instead of placing emphasis on showcasing and showing only best works, teachers who require developmental portfolios look at the progress a student has made. According to the ability of the student, progress and long-term retention are perhaps best reflected in developmental portfolios.

The developmental portfolio must show personal ownership by the compiler, literacy development, and academic accomplishment (to some degree). The portfolio is very personal within the parameters that the compiler and the audience have set together.

The portfolio serves as an archival collection of data and documentation. When the documentation is collected, time must be allotted for the student to organize the material chronologically, from worst to best. If this is not done in a classroom on a regular basis, the task of ordering will be so large that the student will be overly frustrated and learning will be hampered.

The culling process requires students to make decisions about which items may be placed in their portfolios. They cull from a large number of artifacts that they have collected and make each piece that they choose relevant. Often, those who make developmental portfolios bog down in this stage of the process. They will come to their audience and get the teacher or their peers to help them decide on the ordering process. In fact, they may get their peers to decide which pieces to use. As long as ownership is maintained and the documentation is authentic to the student preparing the portfolio, help from others is allowable. If the document starts to become more like a peer's presentation or more like the teacher's expectation, then the portfolio has lost its effectiveness.

The reflection stage of the process is very difficult until the final product has been selected and turned in for evaluation. It is difficult because rationalizing the value of an artifact is what the developmental portfolio is about. The compilers have to understand that if the guidelines for the portfolio require five artifacts and reflections on each of the five items, even after they have selected five initial items their selections are not carved in stone. One may certainly change any documentation if a new or reconsidered document later seems to tell the compiler's story better or more appropriately (the R of CORP). This is where the recursive process comes into play in developmental portfolios.

If some items are chosen to best show development, and another artifact appears that is better, students can negotiate with the assessor to include a new artifact or add another document to help tell the full developmental story. Paradoxically, one of the hazards is also one of the benefits of the developmental portfolio. Once the portfolio is presented and assessed, nothing prevents an individual from later adding new pieces to show further growth and development. The developmental portfolio has to continue to show growth to be correct and effective.

If one cannot reflect on the choices for the portfolio, then the selections made are not appropriate. The reflection is the component that empowers the owner of the portfolio. The choices for the portfolio should show something of the owner in diverse contexts. Artifacts and reflections from outside the school participation context (i.e., other than tests, papers, book reports, etc.) would certainly offer some satisfaction to the assessor. If an artifact or a reflection does not empower the compiler and establish pride in the work, the compiler should reconsider the effort involved and choose some other kind of artifact. A big success factor is making sure the task of compilation does not become so overwhelming that it cannot be accomplished. The teacher must emphasize time-management skills so that time issues will not become a factor in the success and self-esteem of the student preparing the portfolio.

The presentation (the P of CORP) comes when the student gives the completed portfolio to the assessor. The presentation can be oral, with the presenter telling why he chose each piece in the portfolio, or the student may merely turn in a completed project.

Summary

The developmental portfolio is a very useful tool for checking the progress of the compiler from the compiler's point of view. Artifacts for the portfolio are selected and then reflected on by the compiler. The artifacts must show progression in a hierarchical order ascending toward the compiler's best work. There must be evidence that some special selection has taken place to assure that progress is shown. This portfolio works for any capability level; even though the last artifact may be among the best works of the presenter, that work may not be "good" in comparison with others who might be presenting another type of portfolio. The work shown should indicate that the presenter has moved upward or progressed. Progress, then, is the key word for assessment in this kind of portfolio work because the one preparing the portfolio can justify growth through the reflective pieces that accompany the artifacts.

This portfolio will have an entirely different rubric from the showcase or the comprehensive portfolio. Students preparing the developmental portfolio will help the assessor decide which items will be assessed by the rubric and how they will be assessed. In fact, each portfolio will basically be judged on the assumption that progress is made, and the criteria for the assessment will simply ask if progress has been shown from the first to the final artifact.

Questions

1. What are the two basic factors that make a portfolio developmental?

2. In collecting for a developmental portfolio, what is meant by the phrase "Who I am becoming"?

3. What is the importance of ownership in portfolio planning?

Topics for Consideration

1. In a discussion group, try to make a rubric or a checklist to help decide how to choose items for a developmental portfolio. In this group, decide how you could rank items in a hierarchical order if the student was a good student, a moderate student, or a very poor student.

2. Write a special reflection for an artifactual piece you have that is not necessarily well done, but should be included as the beginning artifact for the student who is compiling a portfolio. Be sure that there are guidelines for the reflection, so that all items are written following the same guidelines.

3. Design a checklist to rate the oral presentation of the developmental portfolio. Design one that touches on the same kind of information, but in a written format.

3

Showcase Portfolios
Putting Your Best Foot Forward

"I want to show you my work, Dr. Rodriguez, but I do not want to show you everything I have done, and I don't want to put the things that I think are my better pieces into a somewhat chronological order: I just want you to see what I have to offer. What should I do?" Sarah asked.

"What you are asking about is the showcase portfolio. You want to place five or six of your best pieces of work into a special collection for me so that I don't have to filter through all the pieces you have done this semester and perhaps miss those things in which you feel you are more accomplished. Right?"

"That's it! Can I do that for you, and make sure you get my best stuff?"

"When you choose your best works to show for assessment, we call that collection a showcase portfolio," Dr Rodriguez said, "and the showcase pieces are chosen either by you or by you and me. We can look through your comprehensive collection folder and choose just those representative pieces that you want me to evaluate for your semester's mark. You will, of course, have the final say in choosing the pieces you wish to be judged, and then you will reflect on why you made the choices you made. And that showcase collection is what I will mark."

What Is a Showcase Portfolio?

Like the other portfolios previously discussed, the showcase portfolio is a collection of works selected for display by the owner of the portfolio. The very word "showcase" gives away the definition. This portfolio is the place wherein the owner can exhibit the best works or pieces to set the owner apart from others who have prepared portfolios based on the same general theme. The showcase portfolio is much like a glass display case in a museum or in a department store, where objects are on display for special viewing or specialized sales. The pieces (objects) that are in the portfolio (display case) must have a special viewing (by a professor judging the student's work, by an assessment team making an evaluation of a program, or by a school official who views the portfolio with the idea of hiring its compiler).

What Constitutes "Best" Works?

The person compiling the showcase portfolio has to be astute in selecting the best works from a large number of possibilities, often a comprehensive collection of works done within a given period of time. Preliminary questions that the compiler has to ask are, "Who is the audience for this portfolio? How do I best impress that audience with the selections I make for the presentation?"

One's showcase artifacts can change as often as needed to impress different audiences for different purposes. Because the showcase is changeable based on the needs of specific audiences, one should keep all pertinent materials that have been collected as possible display. Keep these items in a comprehensive file, so that from the comprehensive collection appropriate showcase items can be selected and made ready for the specialized display. A teacher or a professor helping students get materials ready for a showcase presentation should ask the students to verbalize, or perhaps to write, a theoretical basis for each item selected. At the same time, the students should also prepare a written reflection on why the piece needs to be included in a portfolio. By keeping materials and reflections in good order and current, a showcase portfolio may be pulled together easily for different audiences and on very short notice.

One student, Mary Alexander, heard in class one day the old Chinese proverb: "Tell me, and I will forget; show me, and I may understand; involve me, and I will remember." The student typed the adage in the center of a sheet of paper and placed it in her comprehensive file drawer, thinking that when it was time to bring together items for her showcase portfolio, this piece might work. She did use the work and wrote the following as her theory base and her reflection:

> My artifact shows how the prospective teacher should understand the concept of making learning enjoyable. The need for a willingness to change is required when the teacher leads her student to greater learning and development.

> This proverb makes it very clear that change is necessary in the classroom learning environments, no matter how well planned one thinks

she is. The proverb is one that can win support almost immediately. Involvement is the key to making learning enjoyable. If students just sit back and watch everything taking place without participating, they will eventually become bored, they'll quit listening, and learning will, for all intents and purposes, cease to take place.

Hands-on experiences are great ways to get students involved in their learning and help them to remember what they have participated in and seen.

Teachers need to be willing to change their views and their plans on how a classroom works to get higher learning and development for their children.

This artifact shows that I have a strong understanding of the subject matter of making learning enjoyable and a willingness to change if the need arises. When a teacher gets the students involved in application of concepts and ideas, then the teacher has the students' full attention, but if one is not involved, the teacher has not won the battle of teaching every child.

This artifact also show that the knowledge that I gain from understanding the ways students learn and develop will make me a more skillful teacher. Every time that my students improve their skills in the classroom during a lesson, it makes my skills as a teacher also increase.

My disposition as a teacher changes the moment I read such potent quotes. It is necessary for a teacher to change for the greater good of the students. I strive to create enjoyable learning experiences in my classroom so I can promote greater student involvement. This artifact gives the motivation and details to change my choices and actions often for the benefit of my students.

The showcase, then, certainly does not negate the need for a comprehensive collection and constant reflection and justification processes, as one might think a showcase would. In fact, because the showcase does not rank pieces in the collection, as does the developmental portfolio, one can randomly pull best works for this kind of portfolio. The compiler of the showcase portfolio would want no ranking—not even a partial, unplanned ranking—because the compiler wants the reviewer to make judgments based on the overall coverage presented in the document and does not want to portray even the possibility of a growth pattern. The showcaser has already dealt with growth and wants the audience to know that what is displayed are the very *best works* the presenter has to offer.

Problems for the Showcase Portfolio

Because the showcase is supposed to offer examples of a presenter's best works, the responsibility for selling himself or herself lies fully in that presenter's court. The presenter cannot include pieces that could possibly disqualify, nullify, or in any way weaken or discredit the work shown. There has to be a great deal of soul-searching as to which pieces, among many that are possibly available, will best tell the appropriate story for the presenter. When one is trying to determine those "best" works, one has to rely on his or her own judgment to make qualified decisions that will please the audience. The showcase portfolio could easily be the most difficult kind of portfolio to prepare because of that big decision factor. The compiler has to do some astute audience and purpose analysis to decide which items are appropriate and best works for such a portfolio. The ideas of audience appeal and audience pleasing certainly come into play more with the showcase portfolio than with any of the other kinds. The preparations must show a high level of confidence that the right choices have been made for the portfolio collection. One still has to move through the CORP steps and still must spend a great deal of time in reflection. And because this portfolio shows only one's best works, the reflection process requires greater depth and perception.

How Do I Select "Best" Works?

A main prerequisite for any kind of portfolio is the collection process—the C of the CORP process. The compiler should collect every kind of artifact that would enhance a portfolio. Very often this material turns out to be something that is not usable, but the compiler must remember that if one is trying to show best works, he or she must choose different artifacts than if one is seeking to show growth or development.

From the collected materials, then, and without considering the hierarchical arrangement of the materials, the compiler has to make evaluative judgments of the artifacts, selecting those that best meet the needs of the audience who will view the works. A good knowledge of the audience selected to see the portfolio is a necessity when one is approaching a showcase portfolio. The materials in a showcase portfolio are meant to tell the world that the compiler is the best specimen available. The way that the material is shown should emphasize that image. Therefore, one of the most important factors in the showcase portfolio presentation is the selection of the works for the portfolio.

The showcase portfolio should also certainly be a dynamic work, with the strongest emphasis on dynamic. This kind of portfolio is not one that the compiler can put together and then sit back and relax with the attitude that "Whew, this is done now. All I have to do is present it over and again." The artifacts for the collection can change as frequently as one collects new artifacts. Even in developmental growth, as one progresses the work should improve with each piece of documentation that one prepares. The developmental portfolio is more logically set and static than the showcase. If one is trying always to show best works, then the showcase should be updated as often as new, superior work is done. The materials become an ever-changing exhibit owned by the compiler and presenter of the portfolio. When one is showing his or her best side, better, newer materials should be added as often as the opportunity arises.

The showcase collection is carefully designed to reveal achievement. Achievement is the key to the success of the compiler, and evaluation of the showcase is generally based on how well the compiler shows that achievement. If one seeks to prove competency in a given field, the pieces that best reveal the achievement of that competency would certainly be the documentation that one would choose for the showcase portfolio.

The evaluator of the showcase, the portfolio's selected audience, needs to feel an immediate impact of the value of the presenter. Good work on the assembly of the documentation will certainly set up a good first impression of the presentation. A sense of good organization and planning of the showcase must be obvious upon opening the portfolio.

Should Showcase Portfolios All Look Alike?

People know that traditionally those who make the loudest appeal get heard more quickly. That same approach surfaces, of course, in portfolios. Those who put the most glitz into the portfolio's design make their work glitter most, and that glitter attracts the quickest attention. So, a new trend seems to be developing among educators to keep portfolios similar in design within a given area or a given institution, to keep one portfolio from standing out more than another. The thinking is that through this similar-look approach, each student is given a chance to have the work seen in its best light. Proponents of the uniform presentation approach would argue that having all portfolios look alike on the outside helps preserve equality and fairness in competition for recognition among the compilers.

In school situations, this attitude may be appropriate for those who have to evaluate many portfolios because they will not have to sift through mounds of fluff to get to the basic reason for the portfolio's creation. Most schools that require portfolios are asking for a showcase portfolio with a best works emphasis, and if the presentation folders of the portfolios all look uniform, it may result in better and more fair evaluation of the contents because it is the contents that are being appraised. But when a professional person, whether artist, teacher, or stockbroker, presents a showcase of work, there is also the argument that the presenter's personality should be a part of the presentation. That extra "glitz" makes that presenter stand out above the others who are in competition for the position that is open, for the sale of the portfolio's artwork, or for the promotion. Advocates of individualized portfolios suggest that after all, the real reason for the portfolio in the first place is to show off one's best efforts.

Those asking that the covers and dividing pages of the portfolio be uniform indicate that the choice of materials to be presented and the reflections on those materials—the contents—are the only items on which the presenter should be judged. Such a generalization is somewhat true, but for a showcase to be a showcase, even the cover and the presentational style should perhaps reflect the "best works" idea of the presenter. Some folders, binders, or other presentational materials will appear to be overly creative, whereas others will be rather staid and bland. They are all passable and good if they meet the protocol set up by the compiler. The point is that the person preparing the portfolio is best represented by being able to choose the style in which his or her materials are presented. The personality of the presenter should definitely shine forth from the very first impression of the portfolio, and the first impression is usually the cover or the binder of the portfolio if it is presented in a book format. If uniformity requirements prohibit the presenter from being authentically represented, then perhaps the showcase portfolio has not been achieved. It is true that a certain level of craftsmanship and an appropriate professionalism should show through, but creativity must not be stifled in the process of trying to set uniform standards for all the portfolios.

An argument for uniformity is that those judging the portfolios will not be distracted by anything extraneous, and can focus on just the contents of the collection if all the pages have a similar form and if the cover of the portfolio and the division pages are uniform. The judge's job may be easier if the protocol for the collection and presentation is more strictly set and adhered to. Those in classrooms or programs who prepare portfolios do move at approximately the same speed over their classwork. They use the same textbooks, take the same examinations, abide by the same set of rules; therefore, logic would argue that they should all use the same protocol and consistency in the way their materials are presented. A uniform rubric for how the portfolio is to be presented, then, would be adopted and used in the judging of all the portfolios. Proponents of the consistency idea argue that the portfolios should then be easier to evaluate, and that all will be judged alike.

Of course, once the showcase portfolio has been selected as the appropriate form of presentation, each individual prepares the document in such a way as to show ownership. Creativity shows up in a creative person's work—including portfolio presentation—almost unintentionally, whether the presentation is in a uniform format or not. The very purpose of a showcase portfolio is to show one's creativity, and there is really little one can do to keep from letting that creativity show.

Another point about consistency is that with the technology now available, each compiler can design and collect materials and record them on compact disks (CDs), an option that until recently had not been feasible (see Chapter 10). Recording a CD portfolio allows for a much wider range of materials than can be presented in a limited space or limited collection. Many schools of education are requiring students to have on their CDs photographs of themselves in action in the classrooms. Many ask that students put videotapes of their teaching assignments and classroom presentations on the CD portfolio so that evaluators will have a more complete record of the student's activities as a teacher candidate. In addition, CDs are very easily catalogued and stored for a permanent record.

One of the problems with the electronic portfolio is that collectors tend to want to save everything on CD, and it becomes more of a comprehensive portfolio than a showcase. When one can save everything in such a small space, best-works data is much more difficult to define and choose for showcasing. Most people, especially those who are unsure of what evaluators want to see, will tend to be too ready to save and share everything they have collected. When this happens, the portfolios stop being showcase presentations and revert to a comprehensive collection.

Why Would I Make a Showcase Portfolio?

There is not one among us who does not want to impress others, especially those who are in a position to give out rewards. The compiler of a showcase portfolio is in the same situation. If we look for jobs, or want raises and promotions, or strive for higher marks in the school record books as an evaluation of works done, the best promotion that can be accomplished is to show ourselves and our works from the best possible vantage point. This kind of promotion of our lives makes it appear as if we are preserving for posterity those good works that will reflect us for ages to come. All people want to have monumental histories written so that the world will recognize their worth after they have departed this life. The showcase portfolio is comparable to a monumental history of one's life over a given period of time, dealing intensely with a specific area of that life. The compiler hopes that those appraising him or her will be able to see that he or she deserves the best possible rewards based on this collection of artifacts and reflections about the works shown. All people want to reap the benefits of work well done. Whether we like to admit it or not, all of us would like to have a monument of some kind erected to our work, our creativity, and our memories. The showcase portfolio is at least the first step toward that monument's creation.

Gathering data and material is not an easy endeavor on its own, but choosing which material one wants to include as part of a monumental history is perhaps the most difficult part of the task. Another difficulty is telling the reviewer why one believes the artifacts have achieved monumental status in preserving and presenting one's story appropriately and adequately (reflecting on the materials selected). Campbell, Cignetti, Melenyzer, Nettles, and Wyman (1997) suggest that a showcase portfolio presentation will be unique in "reflecting your abilities, your strengths, your professionalism" (p. 67). They suggest that the compiler should keep the presentation simple and straightforward because the compiler does not want to "detract from the work you are trying to showcase, nor do you want to appear as if you are hiding incompetence" (p. 16) by the way the material is presented. The basic idea of this kind of work is to show yourself to your best advantage so that others will admire you, hire you, or give you other considerations that you desire, while still reflecting your autonomous self. Again, through the preparation and presentation of the artifacts and reflections in the portfolio, the compiler makes a statement saying, "Here is what I have done," giving the chosen audience a full picture of what good things have been accomplished. The presentation becomes a show-and-tell about the owner's best abilities to meet the expectations of the audience. One must be sure that the showcase has not only good visual appeal, but also well-displayed substance.

Summary

The showcase portfolio takes more work than the other kinds of portfolios because there is a need to be very selective about what one puts into the portfolio. Those who prepare the showcase portfolio are individuals who have some special types of items to share, and who also realize that they have a special kind of audience with whom they strive so hard to share their carefully collected materials. The portfolio compiler must take care to present the material in a way that will place him or her in the best light for those viewing the work. There is no hierarchy of placement of materials, as long as they are placed in an arrangement that is thorough and pleasing to the audience. One must have a goal in mind so that when the portfolio is complete, one's best works shine forth.

Questions

1. How does a showcase portfolio present one in the best possible light?

2. Why would one not have items presented in a hierarchical manner in a showcase portfolio?

3. What is the role of creativity in a showcase portfolio?

4. How is CORP still an excellent strategy for the showcase portfolio?

5. Because a showcase portfolio shows best works, why does one still need to write reflections?

Topics for Consideration

1. Choose an artifact from your personal experience or that you have created (a lesson plan from a thematic unit, for instance), and write a reflection to make sure your audience knows why this is a "best works" kind of artifact.

2. Given a specific competency such as "The teacher understands curriculum integration processes to encourage students to use critical thinking and problem solving," create an artifact from your own experience and write a reflection justifying it as an artifact proving your competence.

3. Make an argument for using a video of your teaching a real or a simulated lesson for a classroom in your showcase portfolio.

4. Choose an item on the Internet similar to one that you would like to include in your showcase.

4

Reflecting on Your Artifacts

"I understand your frustration about assessing your own work. It is difficult to do, but self-assessment is the first step in getting assurance that your portfolio is good," said Professor Pollard. "You have to do a self-evaluation or self-examination. I cannot make judgments for you as to why you chose the pieces that you chose. I can tell you whether or not I think the pieces are good work. I can tell you whether I think the pieces meet the obligations that we have agreed on for the assignment for the portfolio, but I cannot tell why you chose them."

"But who am I to make this kind of decision? I am just making preparations to teach. I haven't done it yet. How do I know which pieces make the best statement as to the competency that I seek to prove in my collection?" Tom Fuller, a senior in professional education, asked.

"Tom, I can give you a paper-and-pencil test, and that is one kind of assessment. For that kind of assessment you can memorize answers and parrot them back as you think I want to hear them. But it is your reflection and your heuristic evaluation that I really want to see. My judgment on what you have selected to prove the ownership of the competency is not nearly so relevant as why you think it proves the competency," Professor Pollard replied.

The Importance of Self-Examination in Portfolio Building

Ownership of the portfolio is one of the most important facets of the CORP process. The reflective stage is the ownership stage. Without this reflection, a portfolio is nothing more than a glorified scrapbook. Scrapbooks lack the kind of organization and presentation that allow for assessment of an individual.

The reflective part of the portfolio process, wherein the compiler asks and answers the question, "Why did I include these artifacts in my portfolio?" is the part of the process that allows for assessment. McLaughlin and Vogt (1996) note that the reflective process "encourages the students to ponder what course goals mean and contemplate their ownership of the portfolio process" (p. 33). This reflective section of the process is the part that makes the exercise authentic to the portfolio compiler. It establishes the value of the effort that is made in putting the work together.

Reflection is a part of life's regular routines. Not a day, not even an hour, goes by when there is no reflection about our daily routines and our experiences and circumstances. When we purchase an item that is an unusual expense and outside our budget, there has to be a time of reflection on what the expenditure will do to our lives and our lifestyles. This meditation and contemplation about exceeding a budget or overextending a credit card, for instance, causes many people to go almost into a tailspin of reflection.

In another form of reflection, we constantly evaluate our stances on public issues in our desire to be more acceptable to a greater number of people. We meditate on for whom we should vote, what causes we should back, and where we stand. Reflection takes up a good bit of our time in our daily routines, and reflection holds us in line with our convictions and keeps us from being too spontaneous or impulsive. Reflection requires thought that borders on meditation.

What Is Heuristic Reflection?

Heuristic reflection, in the context of portfolio preparation, takes place when the owner of the artifacts reflects in a very personal manner (very subjectively) about why a specific item was chosen, and why it fits a particular need. The subjectivity of the owner is the key factor. Adorno (1989), interpreting Kierkegaard, calls this state "inductive subjectivity" and discusses the search for truth in the inward person. Those who own must "feel their own experience" (Morris, 1969, p. 138). This indicates that the owners of the portfolio materials must first select items that they feel meet the criteria they have set, and they must then reflect on their hypotheses, assumptions, and constraints from their own perspectives (Michalski, 1987). Habermas (1985) argues that inductive subjectivity is valuable for making choices and is ranked equally with scientific thought. Such choices, suggesting reflection, help the adjudicators approve the collections within a portfolio and assure the owner that what has been chosen is good, as long as the owner knows why the item was chosen and can reflect on and justify that choice for the collection.

Heuristic choice and reflection is a way of knowing that what has been done is acceptable. It "encourages an individual to discover, and . . . to investigate further" (Moustakas, 1981, p. 207). The discovery process is a definite part of the collection and reflection stage of portfolio making. Individuals are ultimately responsible for their acquired knowledge. They must be involved in critical thinking to be able to justify their choices and the reflections they have made as a part of their record. The record is the reason for the existence of a portfolio.

Owners must be able to put their works into some kind of context after they have analyzed their audiences and after they know the approach they will take in the production of their portfolios. A developmental portfolio is very different in appearance and stance from a showcase portfolio or a comprehensive portfolio. Because they are different, they have different choices involved in their reflections.

Before a compiler can collate a portfolio, he or she must look at the whole picture, making the portfolio not only heuristically but also holistically approached. Individual pieces are chosen and reflected on because of how they lie within the whole picture that the owner wishes to convey. The compiler needs to combine and test combinations chosen for the portfolio, weighing them against one another to ascertain whether those items chosen truly reflect the bigger picture the owner wants to reflect. Heuristic reflection suggests a kind of intuitive reasoning as to which pieces to include in a portfolio document. Because the portfolio is a dynamic document, this heuristic approach is not foolproof, but the owner of the portfolio does not have to worry about foolproof selection. The document can and must change based on the needs of the owner to best portray his or her needs and goals.

How Do I Know if the Choices and Reflections Are Accurate?

McLaughlin and Vogt (1996) note that to internalize learning, reflection is essential. This is part of the process of learning to make judgments about which things are acceptable, which are not acceptable, and why they are such. Reflection helps one perform better in the future.

Self-reflection is a part of growth, indicating a maturity in making selections about one's own life. Then learning becomes a process, and reflection on the items collected in the learning process, and the sharing of those items, aids in making a person more aware of who they are and how they became who they are.

When a document is chosen for the portfolio and is reflected on, then who is to argue about the validity of that piece of work being used in a portfolio? If one chooses a photograph, a newspaper article, a lesson plan, or whatever is needed to show either growth or best works, and can justify the use of that item in the proper sequence of putting a portfolio together, there is generally no way that any appraiser can set aside those arguments. No one judging the work can help but state that the items chosen are adequate or competent, as long as the compiler knows what was chosen and why it was chosen for the portfolio. The next section shows an example and critique of a student's reflection on a specific competency.

Student Reflection on Competency 12

Competency 12

The teacher understands the process of continuous lifelong learning, the concept of making learning enjoyable, and the need for a willingness to change when the change leads to greater student learning and development.

Student Reflection

The student used a lesson plan as her artifact for substantiating Competency 12. The lesson plan dealt with giving two children a quarter each with which they could buy a tin of candy. One tin had 15 pieces and the other had 5 pieces. The question asked was, "Did the children get equal value for their money?"

The student reflected: "The concept of lifelong was addressed because in real life we often have to make choices with little more information than the amounts presented in the math lesson. Having the candy and the quarters made the learning fun and enjoyable for the learners and for me. From my foundations class lectures, I learned that it was important to reach children with both mental and physical activities. I believe that the lesson did both of these things" (Evans, 1997).

Critique of Student Reflection

Although the student addressed the concepts of lifelong learning and making learning enjoyable, she did not note the need for a willingness to change when change leads to greater student learning and development. She provided few details supporting her understanding of the competency.

The evaluators felt that this reflection did not meet an acceptable level based on the assessment rubric. As evaluators, we would recommend to the student that she should consider whether this particular lesson plan was the best evidence supporting Competency 12. We would also encourage her to use greater detail in documenting the student experience. Even though the evaluators could tell from the lesson plan and her oral explanation that further details were available to strengthen her reflection, she did not include those items in her written work. They suggested that a rewrite of that reflection would be valuable. The evaluators also suggested that some artifact must reflect the other component of Competency 12, the need for a willingness to change.

Based on this kind of response and critique, the following document was devised:

By completing this checklist, the compiler is assured that he or she has done all within his or her creative power to meet the requirements of the portfolio. The assessor can use a rubric for checking the reflections, with four distinct categories ranging from unsatisfactory through exemplary. The categories are easily defined:

Criteria for Your Reflection Statement

Create your reflective narrative by answering the following questions. Be sure to use paragraph style and double-space the material. Use words directly from the competency you believe the artifact fits. As you include these items, check off each and attach this checklist to each reflection you submit:

_____1. What do you see as the purpose of this competency?

_____2. How would you identify or describe your artifact in relation to the competency?

_____3. How does this reflection demonstrate your understanding of the competency regarding:

_____a. Your knowledge of the subject matter

_____b. Your teaching skills

_____c. Your disposition as a practitioner

- Exemplary: The reflection shows that it has involved a great deal of thought and creativity in describing how the artifact meets the competency as stated. It is outstanding in its interpretation and its presentation.
- Proficient: The reflection uses all the requirements of the competency and justifies the artifact, but there are no dynamics used in the narrative to show appreciation of the artifact's uniqueness in meeting the competency. There are no errors but not much interpretation of the intent of the competency.
- Basic: The reflection does address the words of the competency but does nothing to show how the artifact relates to the total competency intent. The material is generally accurate, but there are still some misinterpretations and some typographical errors.
- Unsatisfactory: The reflection does not address the competency at all. Filled with inaccuracies and typographical errors.

Hypothetical examples of "exemplary" and "unsatisfactory" scores give an opportunity to see how the rubric works. Each addresses the same competency.

Exemplary Reflection

Competency: The teacher plans instruction based upon curriculum goals, knowledge of the teaching/learning process, subject matter, students' abilities and differences, and the community, and adapts instruction based upon assessment and reflection.

Name of Artifact: Learning Styles Handout

Source: National Staff Development Council

Reflection Statement: The purpose of this competency is to ensure that educators are using more than a "one size fits all" approach to teaching. In a world where diversity is advancing daily in every aspect of life, teachers should be the first of any professional to adapt so as to better suit the citizen of the twenty-first century. It is clear that every child can be different from the next in many ways, so it is important that teachers plan according to those differences in order that each child has a fair chance at making their own mark in this world. One would rarely expect an NFL linebacker to perform trapeze acrobatics, and one would never dream of seeing a petite ballet dancer as a sumo wrestler; however, it seems that many teachers today demand the same output from their students, regardless of learning style and capability differences. The teacher should set up different criteria for working with the different students while applying a good learning process that fits various needs at once. The teacher must be a facilitator of knowledge and not just a dispenser of knowledge.

This artifact brings to light learning style differences that may help or hinder a child's development depending on how the child is being taught. If a teacher attaches significance to these distinctions, he or she can make a judgment about how each Johnny or Jane would react to certain assignments and be willing to adjust the assignments to meet each learner's specific need.

This may make having a non-traditional classroom a must. A teacher's knowledge of subject matter may still be passed on to all the members of a class. One benefit of my knowing how to differentiate learning styles will be to enable ensemble groups to work well together to develop a better blend of learning. I can then work out groups who will be compatible for the various assignments that must be accomplished by the students in that class.

The teacher has to realize that not everyone in the classroom learns the same way the teacher does. My teaching skill will reflect this. I will have to use my skills to ensure that each student has the best possible opportunity to learn that which the state mandates.

My disposition as an educator will most likely be a benefit in this area. Although people may not learn as the teacher does, that does not mean they cannot learn. I will have to develop my own disposition and make myself patiently recognize differences and make those differences work to the advantage of the student.

Unsatisfactory

Competency: The teacher plans instruction based upon curriculum goals, knowledge of the teaching/learning process, subject matter, students' abilities and differences, and the community, and adapts instruction based upon assessment and reflection.

Name of Artifact: Learning Styles Handout
Source: Dr. Cane's *The Art of Teaching Classroom*
Reflection Statement: This competency talks about the learning process. It says that student's abilities have to be known in the community and that a teacher has to change his lesson plan to fit the kids described in the chart.

It is important to know that kids are different and come from different backgrounds. When I lecture to them, I ought to make the lecture easy to understand by everyone of the kids listening to it. The analytic ones can take better notes and share them with the other three styles.

I have to know my subject if they are going to get the notes good. I have to change my notes to sound like the language that the kids today use. It will affect my disposition if my students can't make good grades after I know which area of learning style they have in a class.

Summary

As the owner of a portfolio, you are the person responsible for choosing what will go into the portfolio. Inductive subjectivity makes both the choices and the reflection truly your work. If your reflection shows concern for the goals you are trying to reach, you will be able to lend credibility to the goals set for the reflection and the standards set for you. As long as what you choose meets the needs of those who will judge your work, and as long as the artifacts are pertinent to your application of knowledge, you decide what is included. These artifacts should definitely address your knowledge, your skills, and your dispositions, and how they have developed as a result of writing the reflections for your portfolio.

Questions

1. What is the importance of a well-written reflection?

2. The well-written reflection should contain what kinds of statements?

3. What is meant by "heuristic reflection"?

4. What is the basic justification for including an artifact in a portfolio?

Topics for Consideration

1. Rewrite the unsatisfactory reflection above so that it rates a higher score.

2. Find three appropriate artifacts for a portfolio; write an exemplary reflection for each and have a peer assessment of those reflections.

5

Mapping Out the Plan

Jamie was relieved to have finally reached the point where he was taking his professional teacher education courses. During the first day, as professors began to explain their course assignments, he kept hearing, "You may want to include this in your portfolio," and the words "artifacts" and "rubrics." It seemed that each of his classes was going to require many assignments, some of which might be used for this thing called a "portfolio," but as yet, no one had explained exactly how these things were going to come together.

They talked about documenting clinical experiences, writing philosophies, even recording recreational and volunteer activities. Jamie was confused. He wondered how past experiences, present activities, and future goals could ever be compiled into one document. How was he ever going to decide what to include? How much time was he going to have to spend getting this information together? He hoped that someone would explain exactly how he should go about planning and organizing this portfolio. Since he had never seen one, how was he going to create one?

Portfolios, like people, are very diverse. Some communicate information by being straightforward, cut-and-dried, to the point, concise, and abbreviated. Others are expressive, detail-oriented, comprehensive, and lengthy. Because each portfolio is unique, the formula for planning portfolios must be universal, yet individualized; simple, yet complex; orderly, yet flexible. Portfolios reflect not only what the institution mandates as important, but they also allow each individual to take the portfolio clay and mold it into something uniquely fitting that person. An initial question must be asked such as, "How is this portfolio going to be used?" or "What is the portfolio's purpose?"

Determine the Purpose

Before compiling information, it is vital to develop a clear understanding of the intended use of the portfolio. The purpose, more than any other factor, will drive the content and organization of the document. Reasons portfolios are developed include the following:

- To show growth and development over a period of time
- To showcase best work
- To provide information to prospective employers about job skills
- To determine whether program goals or certification requirements have been met

Once the purpose has been established, the planning phase can begin. When deciding what to include in the portfolio, one must ask, "What am I required to include in this document?" If a portfolio is being developed to meet class or program requirements, then there will be specific items that are mandated for inclusion. The student may have a great deal of latitude or very little. As national standards become more and more important, conforming to them is an integral part of portfolio planning and development (see Chapter 10).

Required Portfolio Items

Some institutions require a very structured and sequential list of portfolio items, whereas others allow greater flexibility. Often, a generic form is presented to the entire student body and each departmental discipline develops its own criteria for the portfolio. Other schools of thought require that the portfolio be centered on students' understanding of competencies, and they want verification of knowledge of those competencies (see Resource B).

The National Board for Professional Teaching Standards (NBPTS), for example, requires very specific assessment items that allow teachers to present samples of their classroom practice over a specified time period. The early childhood educator or generalist must include five portfolio entries with the following general headings:

1. Introduction to Your Classroom Community: Teachers must show time and classroom management skills as well as a written commentary and a videotape.

2. Reflecting on Teaching and Learning Sequence: Teachers submit a written commentary and artifacts that demonstrate children's growth and learning within a theme drawn from at least two content areas.

3. Engaging Children in Science Learning: Teachers are asked to highlight an investigation of a science concept. Written commentaries as well as a videotape segment are to be included.

4. Examining a Child's Literacy Development: Teachers are asked to present ways in which they foster literacy development in their classroom. Student work samples and steps they would take to support the child's literacy growth, as well as a written commentary, are to be included.

5. Documented Accomplishments: Teachers are to document work outside the classroom with families and in the profession. Two summaries, including one for accomplishments with families and one for accomplishments in the profession, are required. (NBPTS, 1998)

Common Features

Researchers have described several essential features of a teaching portfolio. Their lists indicate that a portfolio collection should be purposeful, selective, diverse, ongoing, reflective, and collaborative. The artifacts generally are structured around professional standards and individual and university goals. Each of the standards may have several competency indicators.

The competency, indicators, captions, and written commentary should accompany each portfolio artifact so the reader understands why the artifact was included. In an electronic portfolio (see Chapter 9) hyperlinks can be created to connect the items, but with a paper portfolio it is risky to assume a reader will make the connection between the artifact and the competency. For example, if a picture of a bulletin board is included in the portfolio, the student must clearly explain the reason for it. Does it demonstrate a philosophy of student-centered classrooms? Does it reflect the importance of a stimulating, interactive environment? Does the bulletin board manifest the across-the-curriculum strategy linking math and science? Students need to inform the reader how the particular document demonstrates the professional standard or competency. The following is a summary of East Central University student Terry Sanders' opening statement in support of a media technology requirement:

I have chosen to demonstrate my competency in media technology because I have gained quite a bit of knowledge in this area that will prove invaluable as a teacher. I've learned how to operate a photocopier that shrinks and enlarges. Having the copier available at my home has allowed me to share copies with friends and for emergency times during my student teaching.

I consider myself computer literate, having purchased a personal computer 5 years ago and 3 years later adding a second computer with a CD-ROM. The following programs are available to me: Grolier Encyclopedia, On the Menu Cookworks, Desktop Magic: The Ultimate Clip-Art Library, U.S. World Atlas, World Atlas, My Family Tree, and a Greetings Workshop.

In January 1996, I purchased a modem and went "on-line." We have full access to the Internet and e-mail. I have used e-mail to contact professors, friends, and family as well as other educators across the United States. The Internet has provided many areas of research during my college career as well as aided me in compiling many different lesson plans for future use. A word search program was purchased and an electronic grade book program has been downloaded. I've learned many instructional uses for the computer and the Internet.

I am proficient in Corel Word Perfect and was coeditor of a student newsletter. Currently, I've collected 11 disks of graphics; many of those downloaded from the Internet.

To document the previously mentioned information, I've included samples of papers done using the computer, e-mail, and downloads from the Internet. This portfolio is also proof since it was also done on the computer. I've also included a disk of clip art, the grading program, and the word search program I'm currently considering using in my classroom. (Sanders, 1997)

Variety Is Vital

The portfolio should include a variety of carefully selected items of teacher and student work illustrating key competency indicators. Each artifact must be accompanied by captions and written reflections that explain the contents. Including a teacher-made test without explanation is not enough. Within a subdivision on assessment, the compiler should provide diverse supporting captions and reflections, including information about his or her ability to (a) develop an assessment philosophy, (b) compose a test that meets state or district guidelines for the curriculum area, (c) design a grading scale, (d) analyze the scores, (e) demonstrate how individual differences were met, and (f) reflect through a self-analysis of the entire process.

The portfolio allows the reader to understand the complex thinking behind the teaching process. By linking theory and application, documentation of sound instruction is enhanced, providing the plan for professional reflection and growth. Self-analysis is crucial because evaluation of teachers is frequently a yearly "duty," generally designed for promotion or non-renewal rather than teacher improvement. Knowing why a particular lesson was effective or ineffective is essential for continued success and further improvement.

Typical Portfolio Items

Although each organization has its own guidelines for portfolio development, some commonalities can be found. The following are items typically required during the portfolio development process:

1. Introductory letter

2. Table of contents

3. Resume

4. Transcript

5. Formal evaluations
   a. Clinical teaching experiences
   b. Student teaching
   c. Self-evaluation/reflection
   d. Supervising teacher
   e. Administrator (if experienced teacher)

6. Philosophies
   a. Teaching
   b. Discipline/classroom management
   c. Parent involvement
   d. Assessment
   e. Multicultural

7. Letters of recommendation

8. Competencies or standards

9. Videotape of teaching

10. Personal accomplishments/autobiography

11. Student work samples

Though various categories may be required, selection of the artifacts that best support the individual category is left to the student's discretion. Early in the teaching program, students should begin collecting all artifacts that are indicative of educational growth.

The difference between a portfolio and resume is that the portfolio provides the "proof" that these skills or experiences exist. Essential to portfolio development is documentation. If a preservice teacher's philosophy states that all children can learn, then the portfolio should provide the proof that the individual acted on that belief. That proof could be demonstrated through lesson plans, adaptations made for individual students, notes from students and parents, IEPs, teaching evaluations, personal reflections, or even a videotaped teaching segment. Show me. Prove it. That process makes a portfolio different from other evaluations.

Optional Portfolio Items

A second question to ask when planning a portfolio is, "What items do I want to include?" These could be additional artifacts that present information about individual qualifications or experiences that do not fit into other required categories. A word of warning: be selective. Including too much information can be as damaging as including too little. Busy people will be reviewing the documents, so include only those artifacts showcasing skills that relate to the original purpose.

Sometimes optional items are listed as additional information or personal accomplishments. When answering a job advertisement, adapt the portfolio and cover letter to align with the skills or credentials sought. Tailoring the portfolio and resume to meet individual employer needs increases the likelihood of getting an interview.

For example, if you are applying for a job as an assistant football coach and you have spent the last four years working as a volunteer student coach at a junior high school, that would be pertinent to the job description. If the application does not include a place for volunteer or community service, adding your experience in the resume or portfolio may provide a needed advantage, especially if all applicants are equal with regard to years of experience. An endorsement letter from the coach should also be included, as it validates expertise, interpersonal skills, and personal qualities. A team photograph or local news article mentioning your name would also record that experience.

Documenting educational experiences is vital to portfolio development. Without documentation and reflection, the final result will only be a scrapbook or a glorified resume. Thinking seriously about past experiences and how those relate to the educational setting is necessary (see Chapter 6). These past experiences shape philosophies, behaviors, and attitudes. They also provide preservice and novice teachers with a wealth of real teaching skills.

Other Teaching Portfolio Artifacts

Keep in mind that the portfolio is not just a collection, but rather a selection. The items typically included are chosen to showcase skills. Unless the teaching portfolio is purely developmental in nature, it contains pieces to represent the very best of each category.

The portfolio may be thought of as a tool to assist in blending theories and practices of teaching and learning. No rigid rules or guidelines exist as to what or how much to include in a portfolio. The primary objective is first to collect and then to select, including only those items that reflect competencies or individual goals. When using classroom-produced artifacts, however, one must be careful to protect the confidentiality and privacy of individual students.

The portfolio provides a representation of one's growth as an educator and establishes a foundation for goal setting, reflection, and introspection. The portfolio may provide the basis for determining the student's progress in, and completion of, the program.

The following list is not intended to be exhaustive, and the final determination of portfolio contents lies with the individual portfolio compiler. Although most items in the list could be used by a beginning or an experienced teacher, items indicated with an asterisk (*) are primarily for experienced teachers.

Artifacts from Oneself

1. Cover letter: a written statement describing the contents of the portfolio and how the contents demonstrate the achievement of the goals.

2. Philosophies: statement of beliefs including, but not limited to, philosophy of teaching, philosophy of parent involvement, multicultural statement, philosophy of reading, philosophy of discipline, and philosophy of the use of technology.

3. Transcripts: one from each college or university attended.

4. Resume: objective, educational background (certification test results, if passed; state license, if granted), *work/teaching experience (tutoring, student teaching, grade levels, hours of public school activities/ observations, professional workshops attended, volunteer activities involving children), organizations, honors, references (designate relationship to each reference, such as supervising teacher, *principal, university advisor).

5. Goals: program, professional, and personal (both long- and short-term). Include plans for continued professional development.

6. Self-assessments/reflections: narratives that demonstrate self-analysis of teaching techniques and steps taken to improve.

7. Videotape or audiotape of teaching segment with reflective narrative.

8. Copies of teaching materials: include different types of teaching materials and evaluative instruments developed.

9. Lesson plans: highlight with captions the particular areas included, such as provisions for cooperative learning, higher-order thinking activities, provisions for individual differences, linkage to state learner outcomes, and so forth.

10. Case studies: *in-depth individual study, tutoring experiences.

11. Photographs: interactive bulletin boards; student projects; learning centers; informal classroom shots; action photos; artistic models or paintings; things that demonstrate interaction with students, faculty, or community.

12. Professional development: list of workshops and conferences attended, *special areas of expertise or training, subscriptions to professional journals and organizations, self-initiated visits/volunteerism, and substitute teaching experiences.

13. Record of innovative methods: new strategies or programs implemented such as team teaching, cross-curriculum activities, peer tutoring program, and so forth.

14. Record-keeping artifacts: rubrics, checklists, grade book excerpts, anything that documents ability to manage or assess students' progress.

15. Assessment examples: various types of tests such as objective, multiple choice, true/false, matching, essay; rubrics; contracts; participation; and various forms of alternative assessment used to evaluate student progress.

16. Parent communication materials: sample parent newsletters; report cards, progress reports, notes sent home with individual students; parent-teacher conference schedules; parent volunteer activities initiated.

17. Professional writing: anything published.

18. Educational travel: appropriate if travel correlates with teaching assignment.

19. Technological activities: samples or disks including electronic grade book, grade analysis sheet, templates for lesson plans, copies of favorite Web sites including students' sites to be used for instruction, printouts of Internet research or Web pages developed, a lesson that shows how computers or the Internet will be used to enhance instruction.

20. Evidence of commitment to diversity: description of multicultural experiences including experiences with languages other than English, travel, volunteer experience, or work experience with other cultures.

21. *Statement of teaching responsibilities: list of courses taught including syllabi, recent evidence of classroom activities, and personal teaching style.

22. Description of current scholarship: documented artifacts such as self-reflective narratives; *list of presentations at scholarly meetings; awards and recognition; *funded grant proposals; other evidence of contributions to students, programs, and other professionals.

Artifacts from Others

1. Formal evaluations: *evidence from administrators, supervising teachers, peers, and students evaluating teaching and assessment, human relations, professionalism, and classroom management.

2. Informal critiques: samples of assignments with written comments from instructors or peers.

3. Solicited and unsolicited endorsements: letters of recommendation, letters/notes from students, peers, supervisors, and faculty that document demonstrated commitment to high educational or personal standards.

4. Media: newspaper or magazine articles that validate activities and professional and personal self-development.

5. Honors: scholarships or grants received, teaching awards, leadership roles in professional organizations, community service awards, or nominations for exceptional achievement.

6. Additional credentials: *certified trainer for various educational programs.

Products of Excellent Teaching

A word of caution: When including student work in the portfolio, keep in mind the Family Educational Rights and Privacy Act (1974) guidelines for confidentiality. If you share the portfolio with others, then confidentiality of any written materials should be maintained. Student names should be removed when using personal samples.

1. Pre/post student scores demonstrating improvement.

2. Record of students who demonstrate success in later endeavors.

3. Letters that justify the importance of one's influence.

4. Committee or task force assignments resulting from instructional innovation.

5. Positive comparative analysis of student attitudes toward learning "before and after."

6. Invitations to make presentations in area of expertise.

7. Student work that demonstrates a high degree of understanding of the scientific process or concepts, analysis/awareness of social studies, and that integrates mathematical or technological concepts.

Contributions to Personal and Professional Growth

The experience of documenting one's own activities and considering their meaning as part of one's total growth places responsibility where it most properly lies—with the learner. Further, portfolio assessment permits inclusion of experiences ranging far beyond those possible within the space and time confines of the classroom. (Geltner, 1993, p. 140)

The portfolio is an opportunity to gather evidence of developing teaching skills and to reflect on personal growth. As the time approaches for the culminating portfolio presentation, the collection of documents, reflective papers, and artifacts should confirm for the presenter and others a comprehensive and sophisticated understanding of the teaching process.

Collection

Documenting professional growth in a portfolio format requires special methods for collecting various artifacts. The cardinal rule is to keep everything. As administrators are frequently reminded, "If it isn't documented, it didn't happen." The priority then is first to collect, then select. Accumulating "evidence" is the beginning of the professional portfolio.

Timeline of Portfolio Development

While gathering information, consider the following timeline:

Collect and document all experiences. Save all returned assignments. Keep all evaluations of teaching, observing, and so forth. Take pictures of items or activities that would not fit in a traditional portfolio such as artwork, a teacher-created game or bulletin board, and time spent working with students. Assemble in boxes, file folders, or on computer disks.

Determine what standards are to be met in the portfolio.

Select appropriate artifacts that support the standards.

Think about selected items. Talk to others about items and their appropriateness. Change if necessary.

Develop an outline of materials to include both mandatory and optional artifacts.

Think about your philosophies and write them down.

Determine the method of organization and develop a table of contents.

Put all materials together in file folders according to your table of contents.

Get feedback from others regarding the contents.

Proofread. Proofread. Proofread.

Assemble everything as a professional product.

Prepare for presentation.

Share the portfolio with others.

Keep adding to your "self-portrait" of documentation.

Many students choose to keep assignments, articles, critiques, time logs, evaluations, and photos all together in one central location, most usually a cardboard box, and frequently under the bed or in the car trunk. Because of time constraints, the material is saved, albeit in a haphazard fashion, for future use.

Other students keep materials together in notebooks with pocket fillers holding bulkier items such as videotapes and audiotapes, games, and teaching units. The notebooks are labeled with the course name, and students associate the contents of the notebook with the course requirements.

"Type A" students file each project in alphabetical order in a filing cabinet or accordion file folder. Some who really understand how the portfolio is put together organize their collection based on the teacher education program competencies. For example, items that provide documentation for professional growth are filed under the professionalism competency. Here, one would find past conference booklets, flyers of speeches attended, newspaper articles about the conferences, professional development attendance verification, and the like. Invitations and cards representing membership in scholarly organizations also would be filed there. Service in education-related clubs would be documented. Any photos taken at these events also would be included, with the name of the event and the date on the back.

During the collection phase, portfolio materials can be stored using any method that suits the compiler. The goal, however, is retrieval when needed. Some students prefer thumbing through everything before finding the artifact they need, whereas others prefer to narrow down and categorize their collection prior to the search for the right document.

The process of portfolio development is organic. It changes daily with the individual compiler's needs and interests. The goal of all development, however, is to assist students and faculty to submit appropriate and relevant materials.

Selection

Assisting students and teachers to select appropriate artifacts is an important part of the portfolio process. When the portfolio is based on specific standards that highlight and demonstrate teaching skills, a portfolio planner can be used (see Resource D).

The planner is used to aid compilers in (a) describing the evidence to be submitted for each competency, (b) demonstrating how the evidence reflects their learning, and (c) validating how that knowledge affected their behavior.

Planners are used collaboratively during individual and small group conferences with peers and faculty advisers. They serve as a written focus or a plan for fine-tuning selected artifacts to determine their appropriateness, and also as a benchmark with required signatures and dates to prevent last-minute cramming. Often, the professional exchanges between students and faculty assist students to examine their contributions in a scholarly and insightful manner. Requiring documentation of both theory and application to link with the artifacts is often overwhelming, so the collaborative efforts and support of all involved parties are of great benefit.

Many students have reported difficulties in making connections between required activities, theory, and practice, and then applying them to specific criteria such as the required program competencies. The process demands analysis, synthesis, comparison, categorization, and creativity to demonstrate a thoughtful, deliberate plan. Although few educators would debate its importance, this process is not usually embedded in our student evaluations. Perhaps the infrequency of such rigorous assessment is the reason students experience such difficulty.

The following is the result of one student's journey toward completion of her first step in formally documenting a required program competency at East Central University, Ada, Oklahoma. Jama Hutchins' Instructional Competency I Portfolio Sample includes the integration of artifacts, theory, and application.

Competency 12

The teacher understands the process of continuous lifelong learning, the concept of making learning enjoyable, and the need for a willingness to change when the change leads to greater student learning development.

Artifact for Competency 12

The following photographs represent a learning center designed for my Methods of Elementary Science class. I presented it to Mrs. Deborah Berry's third-grade students at Hanna Elementary on April 28, 1997. I included it as an artifact for Competency 12 because I feel it supports the concept of making learning enjoyable and shows the need for a willingness to change when the change leads to greater student learning and development.

Theory for Competency 12

The use of centers in the classroom is an excellent way to gauge the effectiveness of learning. Successful learning comes from doing, and centers can provide this opportunity. Centers may be used as a self-selected activity, a follow-up to a teacher's lesson, an activity in place of a regular assignment, or as an enrichment activity. Centers also encourage children to make decisions and to think independently. These types of activities are welcome changes in most classrooms, and children enjoy them immensely. Using centers enables a teacher to identify easily any problems with subject matter or content. Children have different learning styles and strengths, and the better suited your lessons are to those varying styles, the better your students will be able to learn. Centers allow for modifications to be made when necessary and are relatively easy to implement. Students take an active role in their learning in these types of activities and welcome the opportunity to experience something new and exciting.

In researching this subject, the consensus seems to favor the use of centers. In the textbook *Early Childhood Education,* the author states, "Children from infancy through age eight to ten can benefit from clearly delineated, organized, thematic areas called learning centers." It goes on to detail some of the many advantages of using these activities. Some included creating a cooperative atmosphere for the classroom and providing numerous opportunities for the teacher to observe the students in action. This enables assessment and evaluation of activities as well as student progress. Learning centers inside the classroom provide students with a venue to engage in activities that support learning. They foster an atmosphere of camaraderie, encouraging students to turn to one another to solve problems. Again, they allow students to take charge of their own materials and work, while providing teachers opportunities to observe students and plan individual or group instruction.

Application for Competency 12

The use of centers in modern classrooms can be an effective teaching tool. I have seen successful centers in use and have presented my own in classrooms. Centers are enjoyable to students on many levels. They provide a variety of learning experiences and materials, encouraging children to explore, experiment, discover, and socialize in their individual ways. As they do so, teachers can observe differences in learning styles as well as children's responses to various activities. This enables them to adapt or change activities, as is necessary.

I chose to use my own learning center for application of Competency 12. I feel it demonstrates the need for learning to be enjoyable and illustrates the need for change when that change leads to greater student understanding. The students at Hanna Elementary greatly enjoyed the center I brought to their school and asked if I would make them another one before I finished my Field I observations. My cooperating teacher and I did create a plant center before I left, and the students were very pleased with our efforts. The aspect of enjoyment could be seen in the faces of the children and heard in the excitement of their voices. It was rewarding to see the students actively participating in the activities and sharing their findings with one another. They surprised me with the amount of information they compiled on the human body topic. They took the activities seriously and worked diligently on each assignment they chose. This experience was very beneficial to me and enabled me to see firsthand the advantages in using centers.

The center also enabled me to make modifications, as they became necessary, to ensure greater understanding for the students. One of the original activities I chose for the center was labeling skeletal systems. It was evident immediately that the activity was too detailed and time consuming. Instead of the tedious labeling activity, I modified the center and had the children construct their own bone models with basic materials. This was much more satisfactory, and the children did an outstanding job on the task. Another problem I ran into was the use of research materials for some of the students. A few of them had great difficulty researching their chosen topics based on their reading levels. This called for Plan B. Again, the activity was modified to accommodate the needs of these students. The teacher and I provided additional resources that the children were better able to understand. Overall, the center was a success. The students and I came away a little more knowledgeable about the subject and what it takes to make a learning center work for everyone. I feel this experience was invaluable and stressed not only the importance for enjoyable learning, but also the need for change when it leads to greater understanding. (Hutchins, 1997)

This student's narrative reveals authentic reflections about her experiences as she related how she applied the theory of the university classroom to the practical experience of the elementary classroom. Her captioned artifacts also focused on Competency 12 with all components evident.

Portfolio Length

The debate about the appropriate length of a teaching portfolio continues. Some contend that because a portfolio evolves over a period of time, it should be quite lengthy and inclusive enough to show growth (20 pages or more). Others argue that for undergraduates, a portfolio will be primarily used to secure employment and should be concise (10 pages or fewer). Their argument is that principals and human resources officers have neither the time, space, nor inclination to peruse a notebook full of information, tapes, disks, and so forth. Even those who will be using the portfolio to substantiate program competencies have varying opinions about the proper length of a student portfolio.

Research reveals that the majority of institutions stipulate categories, require inclusion of specific documents and artifacts, and often even outline the exact format to be used, but rarely mandate minimum or maximum page requirements. Because the portfolio is a professional endeavor, much flexibility should be afforded concerning the compilation of materials.

Levels of Portfolio Development

The portfolio should be thorough enough to cover the topic, but concise and businesslike in its approach and presentation of materials. One way to determine how long a portfolio should be is again to consider the intended use of the portfolio.

Level I Portfolio: Initial Employment Visit

A Level I portfolio would be used primarily for employment purposes. This portfolio would be given to an administrator at the time an applicant applies for a teaching position. It would include the basic information needed for initial employment consideration, such as a cover letter, transcript, resume, and some writing samples of one's philosophy of education or philosophy of classroom management.

Level II Portfolio: Interview

A Level II portfolio would be used when an applicant is considered as a finalist for a teaching position. This portfolio would be an expanded version of Level I personalized for the individual district, as well as a vehicle to be used during an interview or for showcasing existing skills and past achievements or experience.

Administrative Views

Jacobson (1997) reports that in a poll of more than 1,000 personnel administrators and superintendents, few required portfolios from applicants. However, researchers from the University of Iowa have found that portfolios are becoming an "important ingredient" in the teacher-hiring process.

More than half of the administrative respondents indicated that they are more likely to request or accept a portfolio once the applicant had become a finalist for a position. Some of the most useful items, according to the respondents, were student work, classroom photographs, statements about teaching style, philosophy, and personal goals. Caution was advised about overloading portfolios. Information contained should be "minimal and meaningful" (Jacobson, 1997).

A misconception exists about how much a portfolio should contain. One should not have to bring in boxes and boxes of materials to validate skills. For brevity's sake, after an individual concept has been documented, additional materials can be recorded in an appendix with a resource list.

When deciding to create a professional portfolio, using the Personal Portfolio Checklist (below) can assist the student to decide on the purpose, the standards that will be used, collection and selection, and the length of the final product.

Summary

The purpose and content of the portfolio will determine what it will look like and the audience for which it is prepared, and will direct the manner in which you will accumulate and assemble the information. Selection of only the best artifacts will prevent your portfolio from becoming a glorified scrapbook instead of a documentation of your professional expertise. Keep in mind that quantity doesn't equal quality; your portfolio will be reviewed by busy people who wish only to see documentation of your teaching competence. Determining which artifacts and designs are most appropriate cannot be accomplished without considerable reflection and examination, yet this is a key to an effective professional portfolio.

Questions

1. Why isn't there a standard form for portfolio development?

2. List at least five common components of most portfolios.

3. What is an artifact and why are they important for portfolio development?

4. How can activities outside the classroom be used in a portfolio?

5. Why would an administrator require preservice and inservice teachers to present a portfolio?

Topics for Consideration

1. Answer the following questions from the checklist and then map out a plan to develop and refine your portfolio.

Personal Portfolio Checklist

What is the purpose of my portfolio?

What required items do I have to include?

What optional items do I want to include?

What artifacts do I already have that will support my portfolio?

Do I need to collect additional samples or participate in other activities in order to complete the goals/competencies of the portfolio?

Have I developed a plan for collecting artifacts?

How will I organize my portfolio?

How will I select representative artifacts?

What is the stipulated length for the portfolio?

What type of materials should I collect?

2. Examine the following scenario and explain how the activities could support the NBPTS standards. Be sure to list the standard and tell why the activity might be included to support his (Manuel's) portfolio.

Since becoming a teacher, Manuel has been involved in many activities. He is a member of ASCD, National Association for Mathematics, and his local and national teachers' unions. He volunteers as a Boy Scout leader and also sings in his church choir. He tutors children after school and is a Big Brother. He serves on the mathematics curriculum committee for his school and is a building representative at district events.

3. List your own activities, excluding your classroom teaching responsibilities, and then determine which, if any of them, can be used to support the NBPTS standards. Do you see any areas of strength? Any areas which you would like to strengthen? Discuss these in small groups and develop an action plan that would enhance your current skills.

6

Self-Assessment of the Artifacts and Design

Jenny worked hard to collect as many different materials as possible for her portfolio. She had gathered photos of herself working with children, samples of units that she had taught, and critiques from her public school and university supervisors. In fact, the boxes were beginning to take over her dorm room. She never imagined that one could collect so much stuff from two years of college classes, clinical experiences, and personal accomplishments.

Although each student had been given a list of program competencies and was told to document each one with two samples of their best work, Jenny was having difficulty correlating materials with competencies. It seemed that she could use some items in more than one category, whereas other documents appeared to be useless.

She had learned a great deal through some non-school-related activities, but they did not seem to fit into any particular category. She wondered how professors were going to evaluate the portfolios when each student had so many different experiences.

Were the experiences she had satisfactory? Would she include the "right" documents to support her learning? How could she know if her reflections were on target? She was becoming very frustrated and uneasy about this big project.

Reflect Who You Are

Once portfolio materials have been collected, the real work begins. One must determine how all of these artifacts can be assembled into a shining profile of you: who you are, what you have experienced, and how you feel about teaching. Because the documents will ultimately endorse an individual's teaching, application, and organization skills, materials must be deliberately and thoughtfully selected.

Many events have shaped your thinking about education, so the manner in which you choose to present them frequently determines the success of the portfolio. The process begins with the obvious physical considerations and ends with the final assessment. Does this portfolio reveal the scope of your learning, both formal and informal? Your professional self is mirrored in the portfolio, from the type of paper and design elements chosen to the writing style and selected artifacts. The organization of your portfolio also is a revelation. Your portfolio will most definitely send a message to the reader. The goal is to ensure it is a message indicative of your past, present, and future.

Accentuate the Positive

Students frequently feel inadequate when trying to validate specific required competencies. Because student education experiences are often limited, with minimal classroom time accumulated, some mistakenly assume validation of such goals is impossible. Students comment, "How can I show that I understand curriculum integration when I have only taught one unit?" or "How can I prove that I understand the importance of fostering positive interaction with school colleagues, parents and families, and organizations in the community when I have limited contact with them?"

One way instructors can assist students to recognize their current level of expertise is by conducting workshops, seminars, courses, and conferences where a positive exchange of information and concerns can be communicated. Sharing samples of acceptable levels of work, as well as some that are exemplary and some that are below expected levels, provides a construct from which students can begin to understand the portfolio process.

However limited their skills, students often have learned a variety of skills that until now were not considered to be "teaching" attributes. Small groups and individualized portfolio planning conferences such as portfolio peer groups (see Chapter 2) have proven to be a valuable aid to students as they prepare their portfolios.

Guided Professional Conversations

A necessary component of portfolio development is the professional conversations with peers, professors, practicing teachers, and mentors. Although students have diverse experiences, the competencies or program goals are standard. Therefore each student must assess which experiences will reveal growth or expertise in a particular area. No one can fully know another's past or how that past affected his or her attitude and learning. This step is a solitary examination that requires reflection and thought, as discussed in Chapter 4.

Integrate Non-teaching Experiences

Students often underestimate the strength of non-education-related experiences. Cristy Gilreath was required to validate an understanding of Competency 13, which deals with the legal aspects of teaching: rights of students, parents, and families; and the legal rights and responsibilities of the teacher. She was very frustrated because, according to her, she had virtually no experience in dealing with legal issues related to education.

Using the portfolio planner (see Resource D) as a conversation focus, she was asked to relate any issues that dealt with rights or responsibilities. She then recalled that during her time as an Upward Bound counselor, her job description included many of the legal responsibilities of a teacher. The following excerpt was written after an individual conference with her instructor.

Our orientation consisted of a lot of rule reading and instruction on how to fill out the mountain of forms they gave us. There were forms for everything. Then we were made aware of the legal aspects. These forms were for the protection of us as people with privileged information as well as the students and their families.

We had to sign confidentiality agreements. This was to make sure the students' social security numbers and other personal information were safe. We also had to document all time spent alone with students. For our safety, the director suggested that we keep a contact diary. (Gilreath, 1997)

Gilreath continued by linking her Foundations of Education class knowledge, specifically the Family Educational Rights and Privacy Act (1974), with her experiences as a summer counselor in order to validate her learning.

Before learning about FERPA, I thought that just about anyone could look at your grades. I feel now that I can better understand some of the legal aspects of teaching, including the rights of students and their parents/families when seeking information from educational records.

Document Peripheral Experiences

After one or two portfolio conferences, most students begin to understand how their past has influenced their learning. Some examples of student learning experiences that have valuable "carryover" include the following:

- Substitute teaching: any grades
- Church-related teaching: any age or specialty such as choir
- Civic experiences: Boys Club, Girls Club, YMCA, Big Brother, Big Sister, Boy Scouts, Girl Scouts, mentoring

- Volunteer work: grades preK through 12, hospital or community events
- Counseling: summer camps
- Tutoring: any age
- Leadership roles in social clubs: any appropriate, with special emphasis on education-related fraternities
- Committee work: include role and responsibility
- Supervisory roles: work-related or volunteer
- Presentation skills: speeches, panel participant, presenter
- Clinical teaching
- Student teaching
- Job experience: especially technology, training, or human relations

At times, students need assistance to process and sift through the enormous amount of possible information. Directed conferences held with peers and teachers greatly enhance the student's ability to relate previous learning to required objectives. The hardest parts of the process are the student's leap from the theory to the application and verifying their understanding of how one complements the other.

Determine Purpose and Audience

When compiling information for the portfolio, think about the purpose of the portfolio as well as the person who will be evaluating the materials (see Chapter 3). The chosen documents should reflect the expected outcome.

If the portfolio is to be used as an application for employment, consider which artifacts will enhance your job skills. Will they convince a principal to hire you?

If it is a developmental portfolio, consider which documents support your self-assessment and growth. Will they prove to a professor that you have seriously thought about your performance and developed a plan of improvement, then demonstrated and documented that growth in the requested areas?

If the portfolio is for teacher education program evaluation, consider which materials verify your expertise in basic competencies. Will they justify a peer or faculty committee granting you certification or graduation to the next level?

If it is for individual course evaluation, consider which items meet specified grading criteria. Will they provide a teacher or evaluator with adequate information to show that you have met course objectives?

If the portfolio is for tenure purposes, consider which categories are expected to be included. Will they convince a review board that you have fully and expertly fulfilled promotion or tenure requirements?

Portfolio Evaluation

Many organizations require various combinations of groups and individuals to evaluate portfolios. Some include only individual professors, whereas others mandate a team of portfolio assessors. Some use only internal assessors while others hire outside consultants. Many institutions incorporate both individual and group evaluations. Common education teachers and administrators, as well as peers, may be members of an evaluation panel. When applying for a teaching job, the school principal may be the one who assesses the portfolio. There are no specific rules for determining who evaluates, other than each organization's policies. An exception is legislated state or national mandates for judging portfolios.

One has no control over who evaluates, but one certainly has the option of asking questions about the "who" and the "how" of the portfolio evaluation. Including documents that are important to that individual or assessment team is vital to the success of the portfolio.

Evaluation Instruments

The instruments used to evaluate portfolios are as numerous as the organizations requiring them. Many types of assessment instruments are used: instruments developed by individual school districts or departments, teacher-made instruments, and instruments designed as mandated outgrowths from state or national committees. Some include checklists, rubrics, Likert-type scales, oral and written narratives, formal evaluation forms, and informal feedback. Others assign a point value, percentage, or letter grade to each criterion based on how fully the topic is covered, and still others have a pass/fail format.

Critics of portfolio assessment argue that its subjectivity and the lack of standardization make it difficult to compare one portfolio with another. However, those concerns are somewhat alleviated by requiring specific documents. Yet a problem remains: how to make portfolio evaluation as reliable and valid as possible, given their individualistic contents.

A solution, according to Doolittle (1994), is to use Likert-type evaluation forms based on the mandated items. Then the categorized items are weighted and ratings are combined to provide an overall score, allowing a more objective method of comparison.

Informing oneself about the evaluation process is comparable to looking at a map before taking a journey. Know what is expected and, within the expectation, the various rating levels that are acceptable. In planning your portfolio, familiarize yourself with the intended outcomes. Determine what it will look like, what format it will have, what required categories and mandatory artifacts will be included, and what guidelines will be used for organization, and then personalize it.

Sample Evaluation Instruments

The rubric in Resource F will provide students with necessary information about the levels of portfolio assessment. Sharing samples of each level of development will assist students to gain insight into what is exemplary and what is

Table 6.1　　　Sample Evaluation Rubric

	Standards for Evaluating Field Activities: Observation and Reflection Reports Level III
18-20 points:	Report is indicative of exceptional insight communicated in a creative and accurate manner, applying previously learned information. Product is professionally presented. Documentation is exact and thorough.
15-17 points:	Report fulfills all basic requirements with good written communication skills and is easy to follow. Shows evidence of some reflection on effective practices. Accurately interprets information. Product is neatly presented. Documentation supports reports.
14-12 points:	Report does not meet two or more of the required items. Writing includes some inappropriate or insignificant comments. Not enough information gathered for an accurate assessment. Contains little or no reflection. Product is somewhat messy. Documentation is evident, but not thorough.
8-11 points:	Report fails to address three or more of the required items. Information gathered is too brief. Contains little or no application of knowledge of appropriate practices. Reflections are inaccurate or shallow. Writing is difficult to follow and not carefully written. Documentation fails to support findings or is too sketchy to validate results.
Below 8 points:	Report is lacking essential items necessary for evaluation. Glaring inconsistencies exist between data and summary. Report is not clearly organized but moves reader randomly with little or no thought to expected outcome. No reflection is apparent. Product appears to be "thrown together" with little or no pride. Documentation is sparse or nonexistent.

marginal. As students practice evaluating the various documents of their peers, a clear picture emerges regarding the level of expertise of each portfolio document. The following sample rubric with assigned point values can be used for evaluating a reflection and observation of student field activities.

Another instrument can be used as the first checkpoint for beginning teacher education students. It is a combination of a checklist, formal evaluation criteria, Likert-type scale, and rubric. The document also contains a compilation of general information such as a transcript, grade point average, and field-hour documentation.

The first level of evaluation is standardized with mandated items and with little or no opportunity for students to individualize. The second and third levels of portfolio evaluation progressively lead students to self-selection of items based on specific teacher education competencies, as well as some required guidelines and artifacts.

Table 6.2   TEAMS Evaluation Criteria

I. Resume

Organization:	___ Outstanding	___ Fair	___ Below Average
Basic Information:	___ Outstanding	___ Fair	___ Below Average
Neatness:	___ Outstanding	___ Fair	___ Below Average

II. Current Transcript
GPA:
Total number of hours:

III. Statement of Beliefs
___ Well-organized and appropriate with high degree of understanding correlated to teaching
___ Adequately developed philosophy, congruent with present level of preservice training
___ Inappropriate: fails to adequately demonstrate understanding of educational processes

IV. Recommendations
___ Outstanding
___ Average
___ Below Average

V. Response Statement
___ Well-organized with appropriate references demonstrating a high degree of personal insight, easy to follow
___ Adequately developed philosophy with basic information presented
___ Inappropriate: fails to communicate pertinent information

VI. Goals
___ Well-developed, precise, sequential, and visionary
___ Accurate, essential steps included, yet lacks personalization
___ Thought process not evident, lacks depth

VII. Evaluation from Mentor (taken from formal evaluation sheet, 4 = highest level)

Punctuality	1	2	3	4
Appearance	1	2	3	4
Cooperation	1	2	3	4
Professionalism	1	2	3	4
Initiative	1	2	3	4
Attendance	1	2	3	4

Strengths:
Concerns:
Recommendation:

VIII. Documentation of Field Hours
___ Exceeded required hours
___ Met required hours
___ Failed to meet required hours

(Continued)

Table 6.2 (Continued)

IX. Writing Mechanics (grammar, capitalization, punctuation, spelling)
___ No glaring errors exist; grammar, usage, and spelling are generally correct; punctuation is smooth. Easy to read with good flow of language.
___ Reasonable control over a limited range of conventions. Grammar and usage problems are not sufficiently serious to distort meaning, spelling is usually correct. Terminal punctuation is usually correct, internal punctuation is inconsistent.
___ Errors make reading difficult. Errors in grammar, usage, spelling, and punctuation affect meaning.

X. Ideas and Content Development
___ Product is clear and focused with (1) shared insights and important details, (2) writer in control of topic, and (3) ideas shaped and connected.
___ Product is clear and focused even though development is limited. Ideas are reasonably clear but not detailed, personalized, or expanded. Main points lack originality and more information is needed to "fill in the blanks."
___ Product has no clear purpose with repetition and limited information. Everything is equally important. The topic is not defined in a meaningful way.

XI. Organization
___ Product order and structure are very easy to follow with information delivered at just the right moment.
___ Product order and structure moves reader without undue confusion. The introduction and conclusion are there but are weak. Pacing is fairly well controlled although too much time is devoted to the obvious. Connection between ideas is somewhat fuzzy, but organization does not get in the way of main points.
___ Product lacks a clear sense of direction and is hard to follow. No organization. There is no introduction or conclusion, and there are confusing connections between ideas. Great deal of time devoted to minor details, making it difficult to understand the main point.

Students can be given oral and written feedback about their portfolio at this particular level. If deficient in a particular category, students should (with the assistance of an adviser) develop a plan of improvement. If documents are kept on disk, students can correct any composition errors so the documents will be error-free and used for later portfolio development.

The initial evaluation also provides an opportunity for individual students to self-evaluate and determine whether they are satisfied with their professional growth. One-on-one, students are, for the most part, brutally honest about their own abilities. Some may even choose to drop out of the program because they recognize that teaching is much more demanding and intense than they originally thought. Others seem inspired by the challenge and progress beyond original expectations.

Respecting the integrity of individual student choices while guiding them to examine their own levels of development provides an intimate look at student aspirations. Many personal characteristics not evident in other areas of classroom

Table 6.3   Portfolio Contents Checklist for Instructional Competency I

The following items must be included, or the portfolio will be returned and an incomplete grade will be given. A check mark indicates that the item was included.

___ Portfolio notebook

___ Table of Contents

___ Divider pages with tabs

___ Resume

___ Current transcript

___ List of general program competencies for teacher education

___ Documented Competency 12
  2 artifacts
  2 theories or rationales (student theory and expert theory)
  2 applications with personal reflections

___ Documented Competency 13
  2 artifacts
  2 theories or rationales (student theory and expert theory)
  2 applications with personal reflections

___ Short- and long-term goals

___ Pre-professional Field Experience Evaluation Forms I, II, III

___ Pre-professional Field Experience Record Form (time sheet)

evaluation will be examined, dissected, and revealed. The introspection and resulting plans for individual personal growth will be evident.

The next checklist demonstrates specific items required for a group of students at their first level of portfolio development. Each student in the teacher education program must include the items in order to pass the course. If a category is not included, students are given an "incomplete" grade until Level I of the portfolio development is complete. The required competencies are the Oklahoma General Competencies for Teacher Licensure and Certification (see Resource B).

In addition, students are required to present the Level I portfolio to a team of evaluators including two professors and a peer. The instrument used to evaluate the oral presentation of the portfolio for beginning teachers is as follows:

Each student is also rated on the level of documented evidence of the competencies. These will be presented both in writing and orally during the presentation.

The levels of expertise should be evaluated by the following:

Distinguished/exemplary (4): The teacher proved exceptional competence through the inclusion of pertinent information and critical assessment of documentation.

Table 6.4   Portfolio Oral Presentation Evaluation, Level I

Use the following scale to evaluate the presentation:

  2 – The presenter did this very well
  1 – The presenter did this.
  0 – The presenter did not do this.

The presenter:

___ 1. Clearly summarized his or her experiences in the program.

___ 2. Clearly indicated important things he or she learned in the program.

___ 3. Clearly indicated areas to work on for continued professional development.

___ 4. Clearly demonstrated thoughtful reflection about experiences in the program.

___ 5. Clearly indicated an understanding of what an exemplary teacher does.

___ 6. Was well organized.

___ 7. Spoke well, using language relatively free from errors in grammar, word choice, and
       pronunciation.

___ Total points

I consider this portfolio presentation: ____ Satisfactory   ____ Unsatisfactory

Evaluator's Signature _____

Evaluator's Status: _____ Peer   _____Faculty

Proficient (3): The teacher included important evidence and documentation to support an above-average understanding of the competency.

Essential/basic (2): The teacher included cursory documentation with minimal understanding.

Unsatisfactory (1) : The teacher failed to demonstrate a basic understanding of the competency.

Additional comments and recommendations:

The next sample was used as an exit evaluation just prior to graduation. The evaluation team consisted of two public school teachers, one university professor, and a student peer. Students were assigned 30-minute time slots to present the portfolio and respond to any questions from the committee. Students were required to dress professionally, as they would during a teacher interview. After the presentations, students were given written

Table 6.5   TEAMS Portfolio Evaluation-Student, Level 4

Check or circle selected level of expertise.

   I. Cover Page/Notebook Appearance
      Exceptional   Average   Below average

  II. Cover letter/introduction
      ___ Exceptional: interesting, appealing
      ___ Average: average information, no errors but no pizzazz
      ___ Below average: too little information, some errors

 III. Table of Contents
      ___ Accurate: neat, well organized
      ___ Basic: some needed information left out
      ___ Below average or nonexistent

  IV. Resume
      ___ Exceptional: outstanding information and organization
      ___ Average: includes basics but not well organized
      ___ Below average: lacks essential information or contains errors

   V. Transcript
      ___ Included
      ___ Not included

  VI. Critiques
      Teacher evaluation of student teaching (This information was taken from mentor teacher
      evaluation and categories based on the Residency Year Teacher Evaluation Instrument.)

Teaching and assessment:	Exceptional	Average	Below average
Public relations:	Exceptional	Average	Below average
Professionalism:	Exceptional	Average	Below average
Classroom management:	Exceptional	Average	Below average

      Strengths:
      Concerns:
      Student reflection on student teaching:
      ___ Sophisticated understanding
      ___ Adequate understanding but superficial
      ___ Misunderstanding of key ideas

 VII. Philosophy
      ___ Well organized and appropriate with high degree of understanding
      ___ Adequately developed philosophy but does not reflect an experienced view
      ___ Weakly constructed, lacks depth

VIII. Letters of Recommendation
      ___ Peer   ___ Public School Teacher   ___ University Professor
Key characteristics mentioned:

  IX. Competencies
      Student-selected (minimum number required must be met):
      School Structure   Curriculum   Growth and Development
      Exceptionalities   Diversity   Instruction Learning

(Continued)

Table 6.5 (Continued)

Media and Technology	Assessment	Classroom Management

Professionalism

Best Evidence (list student's specific entries and support for mastery of that competency)

___ Student shows substantial evidence of critically assessing and selecting pertinent documents and reflections reveal an insightful and thoughtful educator.

___ Student shows some evidence of selecting important documents to support his or her competence in the selected areas.

___ Student fails to substantiate an understanding, reflection, and documentation of the competencies.

X. Personal Accomplishments

   ___ Items reflect a representation of the student not seen in other artifacts, including shared insights, important details, and a revelation of student thoughts.

   ___ Items are limited and lacking in personalization. Reflection lacks depth.

   ___ Items appear to be randomly selected without a plan or an explanation of the significance of their inclusion.

XI. Anecdote/Closing

   ___ Exceptional

   ___ Average

   ___ Below average

Comments:

XII. Overall Review of the Portfolio

If you were interviewing this person for a teaching position, what comments would you make regarding the oral presentation and/or portfolio documents presented by this applicant? (This section was included to provide feedback for students prior to their pre-employment interviews.)

Comments:

A. Strengths:

B. Areas of concern:

C. Consider for future development:

D. Employability: Rate with 5 being the highest

Scholarship	Unsatisfactory	1	2	3	4	5	Excellent
Appearance	Poor	1	2	3	4	5	Superior
Personality	Insecure	1	2	3	4	5	Poised
Educational	Diffused	1	2	3	4	5	Clear knowledge
Disposition	Negative	1	2	3	4	5	Cheerful/ Pleasant
Knowledge of Basic Instruction	Unsatisfactory	1	2	3	4	5	Knowledgeable
Knowledge of Management	Unsure	1	2	3	4	5	Fully Understood
Hiring Recommendation	Do not consider	1	2	3	4	5	Hire or employ later

feedback about the strengths and weaknesses of the portfolio and presentation. Personal conferences were also arranged for those who requested them.

One unexpected occurrence during the portfolio presentations was the emotion that erupted as students shared not only their educational philosophies but their personal ones as well. Many students related that creating and presenting the portfolio was the most difficult thing they had ever done—not because of the time involvement, although that was substantial, but because of the self-evaluation required. They had finally reached a career climax, recognizing through their portfolio presentation all that they had accomplished.

One student said she actually slept with the portfolio at the end of the bed so it was the last thing thought about at night and the first thing thought about in the morning. The unique discovery of oneself begins as documents are collected, ideas are organized, philosophies reflected on, and artifacts presented (CORP). The lifelong journey of self-actualization has begun. Funny, it just looks like a notebook.

Summary

The assessment of portfolios is conducted through various means, including informal conversations with peers and faculty. Formal conferences also bring focus to portfolio progress and motivate the compiler toward greater understanding. Checklists ensure that all components are included. Numerical or letter grades are given to assess levels of expertise. Rubrics are used as instructional tools as well as landmarks of growth. Likert-type scales also are used to accommodate the need for more standardized, objective methods of assessment.

The key is authentic assessment. Valid portfolio assessment must be flexible enough for each individual to include those artifacts that best represent his or her teaching ability. Each individual's strengths and sophistication of thought along the journey should be validated. Variety and flexibility are needed for accurate examination. Professional dialogue about growth and development should be a by-product of portfolio development, and through the assessment, a shared vision is forged of educators striving to fulfill individual potential.

Questions

1. What methods can be used to determine whether an artifact documents a specific outcome?

2. List various uses of a portfolio.

3. What are the advantages and disadvantages of each of the following in portfolio assessment: (a) numeric/letter grades, (b) checklists, (c) informal conversations, (d) rubrics, (e) Likert scales, and (f) formal conferences.

4. What is "authentic assessment" and why is it vital to portfolio development?

Topics for Consideration

1. Which of the assessments discussed in this chapter would you prefer using when developing your portfolio? Why? Based on your selection, what does this choice tell you about your teaching and learning styles?

2. Select a common teaching topic, such as discipline, cooperative learning, parent involvement, or assessment, and discuss the topic with a partner. As you share your ideas and opinions about the topic, determine what key components you each could use if you were to include this topic as a portfolio item. Then determine what artifacts you have that would support your ideas about the topic.

3. How can professional dialogue enhance portfolio development? Make a list of questions that you'd like to ask a mentor about creating and documenting growth.

7

Putting It All Together
Nuts and Bolts

"Okay," thought Juan, "I finally have the information I need to put this portfolio together."

He had it, all right—in notebooks, in file folders, in boxes, and on disks. Some of the necessary documents were in the trunk of his car, and he still needed to retrieve some letters of recommendation from his former employers and public school mentors.

The physical component of the portfolio was something he had not thought about until recently. Now he wondered how to showcase the myriad artifacts he had collected. He did not want to carry a gigantic 10-pound notebook into the interviews, but he did want the interviewer to be impressed with his organization and ability. His portfolio was a physical documentary complementing his talent, his long-range commitment, and the progress he had made during the past few years. So, how was Juan going to turn all this information into some type of logical, well-defined employment tool?

"One thing is certain, Juan. You must have a plan, an outline for organization. Then, you have to purchase the necessary materials to enhance the documents. Next, you'll determine the look of the final product. Finally, you'll have to put it all together. Like assembling a puzzle, you'll do it one piece at a time," advised Mr. Savage.

Begin With an Outline

Putting a portfolio together is analogous to writing a research paper. One must begin with an outline. One must think about major headings, subheadings, and supporting details. One must consider the introduction, body, and conclusion because the entire portfolio will be more convincing if it has a seamless communication purpose.

When attempting to validate an area, goal, or competency, begin by informing the reader of the goal. Insert personal reflections and anecdotes to orient a reader to the supporting documents that validate the accomplishment of the goal. An example of validating the area of assessment might include the following outline:

I. Assessment

The teacher understands and uses a variety of assessment strategies to evaluate and modify the teaching/learning process ensuring the continuous intellectual, social, and physical development of the learner.

    A. Philosophy of assessment: comparable to an introductory paragraph of a research paper

    B. Teacher-made samples

    C. Student work

    D. Grade book sample

Begin with a major heading, such as "Assessment" or some other required competency. Next, write an introductory statement or philosophy that gently guides the reader into your thoughts about the subject. The subheadings would be the individual artifacts that support the major heading. Samples of a variety of teacher-made tests and assignments could expand your original philosophy about authentic assessment. Copies of assignments and tests, including your written comments to the students, might also document the importance of teacher feedback. Including a grade book sample would validate the importance of documentation skills, including dates, assignments, percentage weight of individual assignments, and other factors that influence student assessment. Because validation is so important, be sure that your artifacts are congruent with your introductory paragraph. This will keep the reader's thoughts following along with yours.

Introductory Narrative Statement

The following is an introductory narrative submitted by Oklahoma student Kim Holton in her terminal portfolio:

When developing a curriculum and deciding how you will instruct your students, you must consider several factors. Are your students learning all you intended for them to learn? Are there other considerations or areas of the students' development that need to be evaluated? Assessment is not only closely connected to a curriculum (what we teach) and instruction (how we teach it), but it can be used to evaluate students' cooperative skills, effort, and motivation.

Whenever I developed a lesson, unit, or learning center, I had to consider how I would assess the students. I have found it to be most important not only to rely on paper-and-pencil tests, but also use other methods of assessment as well.

Some of the documentation that supports my strength in assessment includes the following: anecdotal records, checklists (both for individuals and cooperative groups), quizzes, rubrics, and even short activities to check for comprehension.

During my student teaching semester, I also had the opportunity to help students prepare portfolios. They were even given a self-evaluation on how well they thought they were learning. Writing notebooks were also kept in order to reflect the students' progress in their writing.

I believe that by utilizing a variety of assessment tools and keeping thorough records, teachers can better communicate to the parents the level of their child's maturity and academic success.

I have included the following pages in order to substantiate my competency in the area of assessment. The documents include these possibilities: a quiz which followed a week-long unit on Oklahoma, checklists (both individual and group), anecdotal notes, two rubrics used to evaluate student performance in my science learning center, daily oral language corrections, math fact assessment, and bulletin board cutouts used to assess whether or not the students understood the difference between facts and opinions. (Holton, 1997)

Kim's introduction, philosophy of assessment, variety of assessment samples, and conclusion concisely reflect important ideas and artifacts. They demonstrate her ability to create, evaluate, and report on assessment of student progress. Her examples support her basic philosophy so an administrator can see that she "practices what she preaches."

Consider the Physical Characteristics

There are several ways to compile information into a portfolio. Portfolios can be assembled on disk, online, or in paper, picture, or multimedia formats. Even if you have some interactive electronic material, such as a Web page with links to further information, or have additional materials on disk, be prepared to give the interviewer a paper copy with pertinent information. Having a table of contents or an outline of the online information, as well as a resume, can provide necessary facts. Because most interviewers require a paper trail (district policies may require a copy of all applicants' resumes, and applications may be housed in a central location), provide the evaluator or interviewer with a hard copy containing vital information such as a resume and certification credentials.

Currently, however, some universities and businesses are accepting, or in some cases requiring, electronic versions that include videotape or audiotape with interactive components. Designing the portfolio to meet individual employment or scholastic purposes is vital. Keeping documents on disk, whether CD-ROM or floppy, ensures the longevity of the materials and affords flexibility when tailoring the portfolio for specific employers or courses.

Determine the Style

The style of the portfolio should be a good fit with both your personality and the intended use of the portfolio. An artist's portfolio is expected to be creative, sophisticated, funky, or avant garde, whereas a business portfolio will be formalized and follow prescribed conventional business practice in its presentation. The teaching portfolio should mirror your teaching preferences, philosophy, and style.

Standard physical components that can reflect individual style in a paper portfolio include the following.

Notebooks

Many teaching portfolios are collected in three-ring loose-leaf notebooks. They vary in thickness from one inch to three inches, depending on the quantity of material in the portfolio collection, and are available in a variety of sizes, colors, and options. Some have plastic envelopes to accommodate disks and videotapes or audiotapes. Notebooks that have a plastic covering on the front, back, and spine encourage individualization and continuity of design by allowing owner-designed insertions to be placed under the coverings. Loose-leaf notebooks are recommended because they allow one to insert pages where appropriate. Avoid notebooks with spiral binding because they limit flexibility if the student desires to change the format or style of the portfolio. Because the portfolio will become an organic documentation of growth, one needs the option of adding or deleting pages with minimal effort. Leather loose-leaf portfolios with engraved initials are also available, though more costly.

Outside Cover

The outside cover of the portfolio resembles a title page. It should include a title for the portfolio, such as "Professional Portfolio," "Teaching Portfolio," "Educational Portfolio," or some other appropriate heading. The next item on the cover should be the portfolio author's name. One may add an address and telephone number as well. Keep the cover simple and easy to read.

Graphics, Photographs, and Borders

Be consistent in the use of borders and graphics throughout the entire portfolio. If a double-lined or preprinted border is used on the cover, then use the same one on divider pages throughout. Some students have used professionally manufactured papers with colorful borders for the divider pages and cover. This can be effective for elementary education portfolios, whereas secondary education students may prefer a more businesslike style. No matter what is chosen, continuity of design holds the information together and presents a polished, professional look.

Do not allow the graphics to become the focus of your portfolio. The document is not to be used as a bulletin board, and administrators will not base employment on who has the cutest notebook. The portfolio will be presented in a professional setting, and the tone of the portfolio should reflect that environment.

When using photographs, rather than including the originals, have color reproductions made. This not only protects the originals from damage, it allows positioning and sizing on the page, with room for captions identifying the photographs. This method also allows the portfolio pages to remain flat with no protruding edges, creating a more professional look.

Paper

Use a quality grade (22 pound or more) paper in a neutral color. The goal of the portfolio is to motivate your audience to read the information. A fluorescent lime-green paper, for instance, is not eye-appealing and will make the reader want to close the portfolio as soon as possible. Select a color that is both personally pleasing and has a professional look.

Acetate sleeves protect original documents and allow easy rearrangement of materials within the portfolio. Pre-punched sleeves prevent having to use a hole punch when assembling materials; the time-saving factor alone justifies using them. Letters of recommendation, resumes, and other materials maintain their crisp, original, professional appearance. The sleeves also allow the reviewer to peruse the documents without fear of finger smudges or the inevitable tearing of holes punched directly into the artifact. The durability afforded by these plastic covers far outweighs their initial expense.

Font Type and Size

Because the portfolio is a professional document, the narratives should be in standard 10- or 12-point type. Times New Roman font is easy to read and prints nicely, but any True Type font accepted by business standards is appropriate. When designing divider pages, create a template to keep all fonts, spaces, lines, and sizes uniform throughout the document.

The selection of font type and size should complement the paper and the graphic theme that you have selected. For example, an early childhood education portfolio might have a border with children playing, so a childish scrawl font for dividers could fit in nicely with the overall look of the portfolio.

Method of Organization

Chronological

Depending on the type of portfolio, presenting documents chronologically may be appropriate. If one is attempting to show growth for the developmental portfolio (see Chapter 2), then certainly this chronological approach would be the method of organization—from "where I was" to "where I am." In this instance, one would begin with the event or document that initiated the need for growth and proceed to the highest, and ideally the current, level of expertise. However, most resumes take the reverse approach, organizing documents within individual categories with the most recent experience listed first and the past experience listed last.

The key, again, is consistency. Starting with the most recent, and following that prescribed method throughout allows the reader to follow the progression in an orderly and sequential fashion.

Competency-based

Creating a portfolio based on specified competencies, goals, or standards is frequently the method of organization for educators. Because the university or organization has specified plateaus of achievement (expected outcomes), educators must organize their materials according to those outcomes.

The standards for beginning teacher licensing and development, mandated by the Interstate New Teacher Assessment and Support Consortium (INTASC), are listed below. The portfolio must validate competency for each of the standards. When organizing the portfolio, each of the categories must be included, with supporting evidence to demonstrate skills. The style is similar to a showcase portfolio (see Chapter 3), with best works presented for each standard.

- Standard 1: Subject matter. The teacher understands the central concepts, tools of inquiry, and structures of the discipline(s) he or she teaches and can create learning experiences that make these aspects of subject matter meaningful for students.
- Standard 2: Student learning. The teacher understands how children and youths learn and develop and can provide learning opportunities that support their intellectual, social, and personal development.
- Standard 3: Diverse learners. The teacher understands how learners differ in their approaches to learning and creates instructional opportunities that are adapted to learners from diverse cultural backgrounds and with exceptionalities.
- Standard 4: Instructional strategies. The teacher understands and uses a variety of instructional strategies to encourage the students' development of critical thinking, problem solving, and performance skills.

- Standard 5: Learning environment. The teacher uses an understanding of individual and group motivation and behavior to create a learning environment that encourages positive social interaction, active engagement in learning, and self-motivation.
- Standard 6: Communication. The teacher uses knowledge of effective verbal, nonverbal, and media communication techniques to foster active inquiry, collaboration, and supportive interaction in the classroom.
- Standard 7: Planning instruction. The teacher plans and manages instruction based on knowledge of subject matter, students, the community, and curriculum goals.
- Standard 8: Assessment. The teacher understands and uses formal and informal assessment strategies to evaluate and ensure the continuous intellectual, social, and physical development of his or her learners.
- Standard 9: Reflection and professional development. The teacher is a reflective practitioner who continually evaluates the effects of his or her choices and actions on others (students, parents, and other professionals in the learning community) and who actively seeks out opportunities to grow professionally.
- Standard 10: Collaboration, ethics, and relationships. The teacher communicates and interacts with parents/guardians, families, school colleagues, and the community to support the students' learning and well-being. (INTASC, 1998)

When corroborating skills in each area, include only pertinent documents that truly demonstrate expertise. Be selective about chosen materials. If one desires, a listing of other materials or an addendum that supports the competency can be saved on a floppy disk so a reviewer could retrieve them if needed. The documents on the disk should be arranged in the same order as they appear in the paper portfolio. Folders for each category or topic can be created to simplify retrieval and addition of further documents.

Importance to Author

Some portfolio sections require or allow individual reflection about topics or artifacts within the standards. Although some of the thoughts will be directly integrated into the standards, sometimes a separate section entitled Personal Accomplishments can be inserted to include events that demonstrate personal growth but are not included elsewhere in the portfolio. From this construct, items that are most meaningful to the author would be listed first, with appropriate reflections on why they were chosen for inclusion.

Mandated by Organization

The first consideration when developing a portfolio is inclusion of every mandated item. Even within these required constructs, however, the individual has the opportunity to include "best works" that fit the parameters of the organization's mandated items. For example, a resume is almost always required in a portfolio. The individual, however, chooses not only what to include but how it will be arranged. The individual, then, has the opportunity to produce a resume in a variety of styles and designs.

Combination of Methods

Portfolio organization may include more than one of the previously mentioned methods, or even another self-developed strategy that has proven effective. Within some categories, a chronology may work best. In other categories, you could showcase in some type of sequence the artifacts that are important to you. Clarity and flow keep the reader involved, so regardless of the method, organization should be evident. Combining two or more presentational styles may provide just the right vehicle for moving the samples along.

Captions

All photographs, student work samples, certificates, newspaper articles, personal notes, memorabilia, and other supporting materials must have captions. Do not assume that the reader will link the artifact (e.g., a photograph of a baseball team) with a fact that you stated in your resume (e.g., volunteer coach for three summers with the freshman baseball team).

Captions can be highlighted by a different colored text, a different colored paper, or with a colored highlighter pen. They should be clearly identified as a classifier for the artifact. Captions should include the five W's: who, what, when, where, and why. In the baseball team example, one should include a caption such as: "This artifact is a team photograph (what) of the Centerville, Iowa (where) freshman baseball team (who) that I coached during the summers of 1995-1998 (when). We played approximately 17 games, and I spent about 15 hours per week for 6 weeks working with the players. I felt it was important for me to learn the fundamentals of working with a group, and besides that, I learned some great lessons about dealing with parents (why)." The entire reflection and validation for the artifact would be a further expansion of the "why."

Chosen Artifacts

The selection of artifacts is one of the most crucial areas in portfolio development. All education students must meet specific criteria, but how they choose to demonstrate their skills will determine the success or failure of their portfolios. When selecting documents or artifacts, include those that you can validate, justify, and support. Be prepared when an evaluator asks you specific questions such as, "How does this artifact demonstrate your understanding of the competency?" or "Why do you feel this artifact best represents your skill in this area?" or "I don't see linkage between this document and the competency. Could you explain to me how they fit together?"

Imagine that you are on trial for having skill in a particular area such as classroom management. The items in your portfolio should provide enough evidence to convict you. Do not rely on hearsay or circumstantial evidence, but only on objective, cold, hard facts. These verify to the evaluator that you truly understand the standards, and your documented evidence proves your understanding beyond a shadow of doubt.

Ask a peer to review your materials and tell you whether he or she understands the order, sequence, and content. Get feedback from various people, including experienced teachers and administrators. Portfolios are not to be created in a vacuum. The more information and opinions you can garner from sources outside yourself, the better the outcome will be. Ultimately you must make the choices, but weigh all suggestions from respected outside advisers.

Language

Obviously, the information in the portfolio is important. The vehicle by which the information is delivered is almost as important. The style of language, sentence structure, introductory and closing paragraphs, spelling accuracy, colorful words, analogies, and narrative clarity influence the evaluator's opinion about your level of development.

Some students have wonderful truckloads of skills, information, and experiences. Yet, having the cargo does not ensure delivery. Although running the risk of redundancy, it bears repeating. Remember that all ideas and information must be error free. This means proofreading and rereading and having someone else read it again and again (see Resource E). Poorly constructed sentences, weak grammar, or colloquialisms have no place in your employment or showcase portfolio. Just as the physical constructs of the portfolio reflect who you are, so does your language.

Electronic Portfolios

The electronic portfolio is becoming more and more popular for a number of reasons. Terry Wiedmer (1998), an assistant professor in the Department of Educational Leadership at Ball State University, elaborates:

> The use of electronic portfolios is gaining popularity as educators and business people alike are discovering their benefits as a means of validating individual performance. Aided by technology, individuals can develop portfolios by electronic means and create, store, and manage

both products and process for inclusion. . . . The new technologies make it possible to show, in ways that were not available before, what students and professionals working in the field know and can do. (p. 586)

Because the number of portfolio artifacts can quickly accumulate to create a massive amount of documentation, the CD-ROM not only provides needed storage space, but also allows for quick editing. In addition, the flexibility of being able to tailor individual disks for prospective employers or university evaluators provides an attractive option for busy job hunters.

Other advantages include the fact that scanning various documents saves time, and video or audio clips can be included to provide actual documentation of your teaching skills. Additionally, electronic storage makes it viable for the compiler to update the documentation with minimal work. The electronic format also enables the compiler to submit the portfolio to businesses and educational organizations via the Internet. Again, time and expense are saved through the use of electronic media.

Electronic portfolios can use multimedia to present credentials, but the compiler must determine whether the reviewers will be willing to take the time to review the portfolio, and whether they have the necessary equipment. Because teaching requires skills other than putting together a slick multimedia presentation, administrators will be unlikely to hire an applicant based solely on the appearance of the electronic portfolio. As with paper portfolios, administrators or interview committees are more receptive to an in-depth presentation after an applicant has successfully completed an interview and has been chosen for further consideration. (For further information on developing an electronic portfolio, see Chapter 9.)

Mining the Internet

There are numerous Web sites about portfolio development on the Internet (see Resource C). One can find examples of electronic portfolios, portfolio requirements from business and academic institutions, instructions for step-by-step construction of portfolios, research, newsletters, news groups, and commercial materials regarding portfolio development. Before creating a portfolio, surf the Web and investigate some of the sites. Good ideas abound, and one has the opportunity to review diverse types of portfolios, methods of presenting and organizing materials, and evaluation rubrics.

Advice on Getting Started: The Art of Ending Procrastination

Do it right or don't do it at all. A lousy self-presentation Web site will hurt you more than it will help you. Lousy includes: a Web site that rambles or repeats your resume, spelling or grammatical errors, broken links, graphics that don't show up or are too "busy," and not knowing how to view the site on the interviewer's computer.

Start now. Better yet, start yesterday.

Your portfolio is a good start—but it's only a start. Do not just hand an interviewer your whole portfolio. You'll want to groom, edit, and reorganize selected portions of your portfolio for presentation.

Think about the content before you start worrying about design. List the 3 to 4 experiences you would most like to highlight. Write a paragraph or two about those experiences. Write them out in longhand, or type them on your computer.

Once you have your content ready to go, decide how your pages will link together.

Once you figure out how your pages will relate to each other, decide on the graphic elements: colors, pictures, background, and text layout.

Make one page with all the elements you need (graphics, header, footer, body text) and use it as a template (that is, to make a new page, open this page and choose "Save As . . ." from the File Menu). This will make all your pages look the same.

Upload your pages. Open the pages on a Mac and an IBM, using Netscape® and Internet Explorer®, if possible. Test all your links. Have your roommate test your links. Call friends at other colleges and have them test your links. One bad link might make your interviewer quit reading.

Print your pages out. Proofread them. Have your roommate proofread them. Take your page to the writing center and have them proofread them. Writing errors speak poorly of your abilities. (Kalamazoo College, 1998)

There are many Web sites on portfolio development, some of which include a database of schools that are requiring or developing educational portfolios. There is no need to reinvent information that is public domain or easily adapted to suit individual needs.

Time and Money

Portfolios are not tests that can be crammed for the night before. Their very essence is longevity, growth, development, and experiential learning. Collecting and assembling the materials, whether paper or electronic, is a commitment in persistence and endurance. As with any project, what you get out of it depends on the effort you put in. Because portfolios are teaching documentaries, they at times consume one's thoughts, choices, and time.

Begin now to save and document all your experiences. Collecting artifacts and saving information that will support your portfolio is being proactive. This is so much easier than trying to create an artificial scenario, or worse yet, having an undocumented experience, then trying to recreate the feelings and reactions of the moment. Because portfolios are representative of authentic assessment, the items included should be those events that naturally occur in your educational career. Therefore, collection should be ongoing rather than a one-time mad dash prior to the portfolio due date.

Reflection is a difficult, thought-provoking journey (see Chapter 4). It takes us down through some valleys and up on a few mountain tops as well. A self-examination journey is not completed in a single night, but often takes weeks, months, and years. Portfolios that demonstrate that level of commitment and dedication are successful. The sense of pride in one's work is exhibited from the paper to the Web page and in all those documents in between. When a comprehensive collection is assembled, the portfolio becomes a mini-representation of you: it holds your thoughts, goals, achievements, and shortcomings.

The cost of an individual portfolio can vary from quite inexpensive to extravagant. Basic costs typically include a notebook ($5 to $10), acetate sleeves ($10 per hundred), ream of 22-pound paper ($7), divider insert pages ($2), tabs for dividers ($2), disk for storage ($1), miscellaneous printing costs ($5), and possibly videotapes or audiotapes ($7). Color reproductions of photographs can be costly if a scanner or digital camera is not available. The bottom-line cost for a portfolio is generally from $30 to $50. That amount is not excessive when one considers that the volume becomes the keeper of your dreams.

Summary

After the documents have been collected, the purpose and audience determined, and the reflections written, it's time to put everything together. Selecting a medium that reflects the intent of the portfolio is the next step in the process. Whether one chooses a paper or an electronic portfolio, consistency of style is of paramount importance; spend time deciding upon the method of organization and presenting the artifacts in a "user-friendly" fashion. This step of portfolio development will mirror your expertise. Make sure it reflects the real you.

Questions

1. Why do you think the portfolio process is compared to viewing oneself in a mirror?

2. What should be considered when compiling a paper portfolio?

3. How can photographs be effectively used as artifacts?

Topics for Consideration

1. Contrast the chronological with the competency-based organizational method. Be sure to include strengths and weaknesses of each.

2. Design a logo that you think would best represent your portfolio. What graphics will it include and why? Is there a way you can crystallize your educational experiences into just a few words or pictures? How will participating in this activity help you determine the style you'll incorporate into your portfolio design?

3. Why do you think researchers use the term "organic" and "reflective" when speaking of portfolios?

8

Presenting the Professional Portfolio

The portfolio was complete, the pictures in their proper places with appropriate headings. The philosophies were written, the lesson plans prepared, and the evaluations complete. Now Jerry was ready to present his portfolio and prepare for his first job interview.

He wanted to appear confident, but he did not want to come across as a braggart. He had no idea what type of questions he would be asked. Actually, he was scared stiff about the whole process of interviewing and writing letters of application. He knew that if he made one error, the human resource director might just chuck his application and resume into File 13. Jerry wanted to follow the proper guidelines, but how would he know the accepted process in each district?

He had heard some students talk about the legality of some questions and wondered what his rights were. What if the interviewer asked a question to which he did not know the answer? Should he fake it or just admit his stupidity? And how was he going to use his portfolio to the best advantage? Jerry had heard some principals say they did not want huge notebooks filling up their offices, so was all this portfolio work down the tubes?

Jerry hoped that by the time he walked into an interview, some of these questions would be answered.

The First Step

After the portfolio is compiled, the presentation begins. Portfolio presentation may begin as a professor reviews it with a student, or as it is shared with a group of educators. In a university setting, an oral presentation is often required to meet specified program or course requirements. In an employment setting, the presentation occurs during a job interview and determines the offer of employment.

No matter what the setting, the presentation is a vital part of the portfolio process. There are some basic presentational skills that can be used when sharing the portfolio with others. When applying for a teaching job, understanding the interview process and etiquette can ease the apprehension new graduates experience. An understanding of employment law can also boost your confidence with the knowledge you will be treated fairly and equitably.

Preparing for the Presentation

Once the portfolio is ready for the first oral presentation, then one is ready to share it with others. The following are some questions to consider before presenting:

1. Who will be evaluating the presentation? Use examples that will validate your unique skills and also satisfy the specific audience.

2. What criteria will be used to evaluate? If possible, obtain a copy of the rubric or evaluation scale to be used. Be meticulous about including all required items, meeting or exceeding the acceptable level.

3. What is the time frame of the presentation? Never exceed the allotted time. Practice. Rehearse. Know your material, and prove to your audience your knowledge and expertise.

4. Will the format be strictly a presentation, or will there be a forum for questions? Try to anticipate what questions will be asked, what your responses will be, and how the portfolio artifacts demonstrate your skills.

5. Have you prepared an outline? Having the basic points on a card demonstrates your ability to plan. And even if you do not use it, an outline provides a safety net for nervousness, forgetfulness, or side-tracking.

6. Does your apparel and grooming reflect the seriousness of this professional presentation? Wear something comfortable and attractive. Poise and a self-confident attitude enhance any presentation.

7. Is the presentation free of slang and grammatical errors? Be cognizant of the fact that you will be judged by what you say and how you say it. A poor oral presentation will sabotage an exceptional portfolio. If you currently use colloquialisms and slang, practice using a standard form of English. Formal occasions require formal speech.

8. Have you rehearsed the physical logistics of finding materials in the portfolio quickly and "upside down"? Those evaluating the portfolio will want to see what is included, so the presenter, out of deference to the viewer, will be showing the material by looking at it upside down. There is an art to sharing the information in a notebook, but it takes some practice (see Table 6.4, the Portfolio Oral Presentation Evaluation in Chapter 6).

Preparing for the Interview

Preparing for an interview begins with your initial contact with the school. Schools are contacted in various ways such as the following:

a. Telephone

b. Job fair/recruitment seminar

c. Letter

d. Application

e. Personal visit

When contacting a school, follow standard employment etiquette. Knowing who to contact, when to contact, and how frequently to remain in touch can affect your chances of employment. If unsure about the proper procedures, call the central administration office and ask for the secretary. Most schools will provide an employment packet containing application forms, telephone numbers, contact names and titles, and hiring procedures.

Be Nice to the School Secretary

Often, the first person you will meet will be the school secretary. Do not underestimate the influence of a secretary's opinion. If you are rude, your rudeness will be remembered. If you are courteous and professional, that will be noted as well. Polish your telephone skills and greet each person with respect and courtesy. Keep the conversation pleasant but businesslike. State the request, thank the person, hang up. Because you hope to be employed at the school, do not blow it by being too nosy, too talkative, or too pushy.

Do Your Homework

When applying at a school, learn all you can about the school. Investigate. Talk to people in the community. Read the local newspapers, or better yet, read the school newsletters. If possible, obtain a copy of a student or teacher handbook. Familiarize yourself with the policies and procedures of the district. Many districts have this information on their Web site, so check it out. If you know the expectations of the school, you can tailor your responses to meet their guidelines.

We're not advising you to become a chameleon. However, if the district guidelines fit nicely with your educational philosophy, then certainly highlight that fact during the interview. The key is preparedness. Knowing that a district, for example, prohibits corporal punishment would certainly be pertinent to a question such as "What type of discipline plan will you implement in your classroom?" Do not dig a hole from which you cannot jump out. You may also wish to adjust your portfolio's discipline philosophy to correlate with the district's guidelines.

Similarly, your knowledge of curriculum, extracurricular activities, and other important program areas also serves as a springboard during the interview. It is important to be able to articulate your educational philosophies, but familiarize yourself with the local backdrop. "Know thyself," but also know thy prospective school district's policies.

What to Wear

Although most people spend an inordinate amount of time deciding what outfit to wear for an interview, the rules are relatively simple. A color consultant told a group of students that they should definitely wear something that (a) makes them feel good, (b) has garnered compliments, (c) looks as good seated as it looks standing, (d) is appropriate for the particular organization, and (e) has a polished "air" about it.

Appearance and grooming faux pas during an educational interview include the following: too much aftershave or perfume (with all the allergies today, play it safe and stick to soap and water); too much jewelry (keep it simple); long, brightly colored nails (have them well-manicured but average length); unpolished shoes (people notice); outrageous hair styles (purple, extreme spikes, or words shaved in); spiked heels (how would you teach in those anyway?); open-toed shoes (it is not the beach); low-cut blouses or shirts (do not let them see anything below your collarbone); jeans or shorts (too casual); and generally, anything that would detract attention from you and what you have to say. Most educational organizations are still relatively conservative. Your appearance should reflect your awareness of that fact.

Most schools require standard professional attire for men and women. Men typically wear a dress shirt, slacks, tie, and sports jacket. For a very formal district, a suit may be the norm. Women can choose to wear a suit, a tailored dress or jacket, or a pantsuit. Some very formal districts would frown on the pantsuit, but again, know the district's policy. If unsure, ask the secretary or a teacher in the district about acceptable interview attire. Given the choice between too conservative and too liberal, opt for the first.

Inappropriate Behaviors

School administrators and personnel directors are just people. Here are a few things that cause them to push their "Reject" buttons.

1. Chewing gum (or hard candies, mints, or anything that impairs your speech)

2. Giving a limp handshake (look people in the eye and have a firm but not crushing grip)

3. Entering the office and plopping down (wait to be invited in and to be seated)

4. Smelling of smoke (avoid that last cigarette in the parking lot)

5. Calling the interviewer by his or her first name (use the correct title: Mr., Miss, Mrs., Ms., or Dr.)

6. Using nonstandard speech as well as slang (poor habits will haunt you here)

7. Being too nonchalant (insert enthusiasm and energy into comments)

8. Asking inappropriate questions (e.g., "Do I get the job?")

9. Being too casual (do not make yourself at home, it is not your office)

Desirable Behaviors

1. Being on time (5 to 10 minutes early helps)

2. Being courteous to all school personnel

3. Smiling; displaying a sense of humor

4. Demonstrating knowledge of state and national standards and the ability to address them in daily lessons

5. Acknowledging the importance of technology and a willingness to integrate it into classroom practice

6. Showing an ability to think through a complex question before answering

7. Having some knowledge of the school district policies and programs

8. Asking intelligent questions

9. Displaying sincerity, genuineness, and enthusiasm

10. Answering questions honestly; not giving "canned" answers

11. Having poise and confidence despite nervousness

12. Having a "willing to try" attitude

13. Being an unselfish team player

14. Showing flexibility and adaptability

15. Being willing to make mistakes to achieve a greater goal; an adventurous and curious spirit

16. Acknowledging a strong work ethic

17. Recognizing the importance of lifelong learning

18. Being prepared and organized

19. Demonstrating reflective thoughts about personal progress

20. Displaying gratitude to those who have helped you along the way; a handwritten thank you note following the interview will be positively received

The interview is undoubtedly the single most important factor in getting hired. However, many students will never even reach this point in the hiring process because their documents were not in proper order. The resume and cover letter are vital to "getting your foot in the door." If these are poorly done, you may never even reach the interview stage. It is vital that you create a resume that is error free, is easy to read, highlights your skills, and captures the attention of the reviewer.

The Resume

A good resume is no more than two pages in length, and concisely provides a snapshot of your career goals, education, and work experience. It should contain the following information: your name, address, e-mail address, and telephone number; career objective; education (degrees, certificates, specialized training, accomplishments); work experience (military, paid and volunteer work, tutoring, substitute teaching, professional development activities); professional memberships (offices held, honors, committees, speaker, panel member); and references (name, phone number, address, job title). An honors or accomplishment section can be added to highlight outstanding achievements. If a placement file is available, include the name of the university, contact person, and telephone number.

Your experience and accomplishments should be arranged chronologically, beginning with the most recent. If you are a college graduate, include only your activities since high school graduation. You may include work experience prior to high school graduation to show a consistent work history. Use descriptive language when telling about your educational experience. A list of descriptive words is included in Resource A.

The format of the resume can be used to attract a reader's attention. Use spacing, boldface type, columns, and fonts to your advantage. Keep it simple, easy to read, and consistent throughout. Select a color and style of paper that complements the print. This is not the place to be creative with preprinted borders or neon colors. Use standard business colors such as white, off-white, or pale gray. Purchase paper that is at least 22-pound weight, which is substantial, feels good in the reader's hand, and does not tear easily. Pay the extra money necessary for fine paper and matching envelopes.

The resume should be error free. One mistake, and the document could end up at the bottom of the pile. Ask friends and colleagues to proofread the resume and make suggestions about the format. This one document can greatly enhance your chances for getting an interview. Make sure the resume begs to be read by being letter perfect, attractive, and packed with pertinent information.

The Cover Letter

Often applicants are required to submit a cover letter with their resume. When composing the letter, use the first paragraph to introduce yourself to the principal or employment officer. If you know the specific position for which you are applying, mention where you saw the vacancy listing. The second paragraph should answer the requirements in the vacancy listing or advertisement. If you are unable to meet the specific criteria, then state what other experiences you have had that would substitute for those skills. The final paragraph should express your willingness to schedule an interview; include your phone number. A simple thank you and resume or application enclosure concludes the letter. Always use standard business format: address the letter to the appropriate person, double-check for grammar and spelling errors, and use a traditional font with 10- or 12-point size of type.

William S. Frank's CareerLab® (1998) lists some common letter-writing mistakes: addressing letters "Dear Sir" (keep it gender neutral), no signature, spelling and grammar errors, handwritten letters (unless a brief thank you note), using the word "I" too much, faxing a letter when the person is not expecting it, too many "creative" fonts, inappropriate language, letters too long or too short, abbreviating words, using substandard business format, forgetting to include a resume after stating it was enclosed, and sentences that are too long.

Frequently Asked Questions

Although each principal and human relations officer tailors specific questions to the district's needs and goals, there are many standard questions that are often asked during a teacher interview. These questions can be grouped in categories such as the National Council for Accreditation of Teacher Education Standards (2003): (a) development, learning, and motivation; (b) curriculum; (c) instruction; (d) assessment; and (e) professionalism. Or they can include (a) subject matter, (b) student learning, (c) diverse learners, (d) instructional strategies, (e) learning environment, (f) communication, (g) planning instruction, (h) assessment, (i) reflection and personal development, and (j) collaboration, ethics, and relationships (INTASC, 1998).

The interviewee can expect the various categories to overlap, and should be prepared to demonstrate practical application as well as theoretical knowledge of the educational categories. The following is a sampling of interview questions one might encounter.

General Questions

- Tell me about yourself.
- Why do you want to become a teacher?
- What are your strengths? Weaknesses?
- With so many qualified applicants, why should I hire you rather than someone else?
- What do you expect of an administrator?
- What can you contribute to our school?
- What is the responsibility of public schools?
- How would your friends describe you?
- Describe yourself using five adjectives.
- Describe your working relationship with your cooperating teacher.
- What is the name of the latest professional book or article you have read that was not required reading? What prompted you to select this particular book or article?
- What is the greatest challenge for teachers today?
- What is your philosophy of education? assessment? parent involvement?

Classroom Management

- How do you feel about retaining students?
- What is the cause of most discipline problems?
- Describe your student teaching successes and failures.
- What is one accomplishment of which you are particularly proud? Why?
- Describe a perfect teacher.

Development, Learning, and Motivation

- What other experiences, besides classroom teaching, have you had working with children or youth?
- What obstacles have you overcome while attaining your teaching degree?
- Why did you choose to become a teacher?
- What qualities do you possess that will enable you to become an effective teacher?
- Why do you want to teach in our district?
- What type of planning is necessary to teach a lesson?
- How will you determine the sequence of skills that are to be taught?
- Have you developed a unit of study that was not in the text? If so, how did you determine the objectives?
- Does your college transcript adequately reflect your knowledge base? Why or why not?
- How does motivation affect learning?
- Do you consider yourself an organized person? Would your friends agree? Your college professors?

- What subjects and grade levels do you feel most comfortable teaching?
- What experiences have you had working with a diverse population?
- Do you use computers or the Internet on a regular basis for personal use? Why or why not?
- What is your personal teaching vision statement?

Curriculum

- Describe how you would integrate our state learner outcomes and standards in your classroom.
- How will you develop a curriculum that motivates students?
- How will you meet the individual skill needs of students in your class?
- What makes a lesson successful for the learners?
- What things do you consider when planning lessons?
- How would you integrate technology into lessons?
- Tell me about some specialized learning programs with which you are familiar.
- What are the basic parts of any lesson you teach?

Instruction

- If I walked into your classroom, what would I see?
- How does the physical environment of a classroom enhance or detract from learning?
- What is your preferred teaching style?
- When would you use individualized, small-group, and whole-group teaching approaches? Why?
- Describe an activity in which you used cooperative groups.
- How do you maximize "time on task" in your classroom?
- What are some classroom rules that you like?
- What role does homework play in your class?
- What graphic organizers have you used when presenting lessons?
- What different teaching strategies have you used that have been successful?
- Explain the elements of effective instruction.
- How do you keep students on track during a classroom discussion?
- Do you think interdisciplinary learning has merit? Why or why not?
- What are some techniques you have used to motivate students to learn?
- Has inclusion of special education students helped or hurt the regular classroom?

Assessment

- Is it ever appropriate to give a student an F grade?
- Describe some assessment techniques you might use while teaching a two-week unit.

- How will you communicate students' progress to parents?
- How would you prepare students to take a standardized test?
- Name some types of grading plans. Which ones do you feel are most effective? Why?
- How will you evaluate your own teaching effectiveness?
- What percentage of your class do you think will fail?
- Have you designed a performance or behavioral objective for a class? If so, what prompted you to do so?
- What steps would you take before recommending a student be screened for special-education evaluation services?
- How would you design a rubric to evaluate a specific classroom skill?
- Do you keep anecdotal records on student behavior and performance? If so, how do you manage them?
- What are the strengths and weaknesses of norm-referenced tests?
- After giving a test, you discover that more than half of the students have failed. What would you do?
- What type of questions do you include on a unit test? True/False? Multiple Choice? Short answer? Discussion?

Classroom Rules

- Describe your discipline plan and how you would implement it.
- What rules do you like to use in your classroom?
- Suppose a student broke one of those rules, what are some appropriate consequences for breaking that rule?
- How would you communicate classroom expectations to parents?
- Tell me about a difficult confrontation you had with a student and how you resolved it.
- What factors contribute to an excellent classroom environment?
- Name some nonverbal ways you can "quiet" a classroom.
- What would you do if a student continues to challenge you with disruptive behavior?
- What role does the teacher play in establishing a productive learning climate?
- When would you definitely send a student to the principal?

Professionalism

- What things will you do to ensure continued professional growth?
- How will you develop healthy interpersonal relations with your colleagues?
- Are you a member of professional organizations? If so, which ones?
- Do you subscribe to professional journals and magazines? Name them.
- What things will you do to earn the respect of your students, parents, and peers?
- What steps will you take to ensure parent involvement in our schools?

- Visualize teachers who are real "professionals." What characteristics do they have? What do they say? Do? Look like? What are they involved in?
- How will you demonstrate respect for the diverse cultures within your classroom?
- What would you like students to say about their classroom experience with you as their teacher? What do you hope is your teaching legacy?
- Discuss ethics in the educational setting.

Elementary School Questions

- What reading and math programs have you experienced?
- Why would knowledge about child development cause you to reflect about appropriate instruction from PreK through fourth grade?
- What is an appropriate discipline plan for kindergarten? (insert grade-level vacancy)
- Explain how you might teach a "Frog Unit" across the curriculum.

Middle School Questions

- Why do you think so few teachers select the middle school as their first choice of teaching assignment?
- What are some characteristics unique to middle school students?
- Do you think middle school students would learn more or less working in small groups? Justify your answer.

Secondary School Questions

- What is an acceptable failure rate in high school courses? Explain.
- How would you engage high school students in learning?
- Justify to a parent your homework policy (Interview Experts, 1998; University of Colorado, 1998; see also College of William & Mary, 1996).

Situational Questions

In conjunction with general questions, administrators invariably ask some situational questions. The same question is posed to all interviewees and then evaluated. The following scenarios are representative of a situational question:

- You discover that one of your students has been cheating on her homework. How do you respond?
- A student who has been labeled as a "troublemaker" has been reassigned to your class. What do you do?
- What would you do if you discovered that a teacher in your building was having a sexual relationship with a student?

These open-ended questions are difficult to prepare for because they are designed to evaluate how well you "think on your feet" (University of Nebraska, 1998). It is important not to rush ahead to a quick-fix answer. Take time to contemplate and consider all facets of the situation before you speak.

Illegal Questions

There are many questions that are legally asked of applicants, but there are some that are considered an infringement on individual rights or could be construed as prejudicial. Questions that are not legal include the following:

1. Are you a United States citizen?

2. Were you born in the United States?

3. What is your native language?

4. How old are you?

5. Are you married or divorced?

6. How many children do you have?

7. Have you ever been arrested?

8. What is your religious affiliation?

Keep in mind that although these questions are illegal, some district applications still ask applicants to list their birthdate, race, marital status, and other personal information. You may leave these items blank or insert "N/A" if you do not wish to divulge that information. During the interview, politely refuse to answer an illegal question by stating, "I'd rather not answer that question."

Questions for the Interviewee to Ask

The last question in an interview is usually "Do you have any questions you'd like to ask us?" Be prepared. Now is the time to really shine and demonstrate that you have seriously thought about your teaching role. By asking pertinent questions, you can clarify any fuzzy areas and show that you understand the full spectrum of teaching responsibilities.

Applicants who plan questions prior to the interview can impress the interview team with their knowledge of educational issues (Career Development Center, 1998). Asking questions also provides an opportunity to expand your philosophy and share any special expertise you may have. Because the interview is a two-way street, the questions you ask will not only provide the interviewer with a clearer image of who you are, but also arm you with the necessary information to determine whether this position is one that you really want. Tailor these questions to meet your individual needs, but keep them as brief as possible.

- What types of media resources are available?
- What reading and math programs are currently used?
- What school counselors or public agencies are available to help students and teachers?
- Are there district-wide student standards or exit outcomes?
- Will I need additional training to implement existing programs?
- Does the school have a computer lab, individual computers in each classroom, or both?
- Are classes self-contained or departmentalized?
- How much flexibility does the teacher have in regard to curriculum and instruction plans for each individual classroom?
- What are the staff development requirements and opportunities in your district?
- Does your district support full inclusion of special education students?
- What is the district's plan for remediating students?
- What special provisions are granted for gifted and talented students?
- Have any of the schools in this district been listed as "at risk"? Which ones?
- What support is given to beginning teachers in your district?
- What is the ratio of beginning teachers to experienced teachers?
- Tell me about the parent-teacher organization in the district.
- What parent or community volunteer programs are available?
- Describe the student composition in this school.
- Does the staff socialize outside the school setting?
- With what community affairs or organizations do the teachers become involved?
- Is involvement in the local teachers' organization mandatory or optional?
- What responsibilities, other than teaching, will I have during the school day? After school hours?
- What functions does the school and community expect me to attend?
- Are there fundraising requirements if I agree to sponsor a club?
- Approximately how many hours a week will this responsibility require?
- Will I be compensated for this activity, or is it considered a part of my regular teaching duties?
- Will I be working alone, or will another staff member be assigned to the same activity?

Presenting Your Portfolio During the Interview

Although much has been written about creating a portfolio, very little information is available on using the portfolio during the job interview. Applicants indicate that most interview committees and administrators were very impressed by the applicants' portfolios. Heather Augustine, Kansas State University graduate, states,

> Although a portfolio was not required at the interviews, my superintendent informed me (after hiring me) that my portfolio played a big part in my getting hired because she could see specific examples of how I taught. . . . I had included a number of interdisciplinary units and lessons so she could see that I would be an interdisciplinary teacher. This was more effective than just saying, "I use all subject areas in my curriculum." (personal communication, n.d.)

Integrate Your Portfolio Throughout the Interview

During the interview, a wide variety of questions will be asked. As you answer the questions, use your portfolio as you would when teaching a lesson. Show specific portfolio documents to expand your answer or demonstrate your understanding of a specific skill. Do not wait until the end of the interview to ask, "Would you like to see my portfolio?" By then, the interview is concluded, and the committee is typically on a tight time schedule. Use your portfolio as a tool, an extension to elaborate or verify your understanding.

Jean Federico, Florida teacher, confirms that she got her job because she effectively used her portfolio throughout the interview.

> I had my portfolio with me, and as soon as I was asked a question that was demonstrated in my portfolio, I opened the book and showed the pages as I talked. Then, I left the book open on the table in front of me. Two things happened—first, the presence of my portfolio served as a "security blanket" for me. Anytime I got nervous, I just had to glance at the book to remind myself that "I am ready for this interview and this job." Second thing—by the time the interview was over, the people sitting around the table were practically bursting with curiosity to see what was in the rest of the book. (personal communication, n.d.)

Administrative Uses of Teaching Applicants' Portfolios

According to the University of Northern Iowa's (1998) online portfolio handbook, there are three ways that prospective employers use portfolios: (a) they do not require one and do not wish to see one, (b) they do not require one but will look at documents as presented by the applicant, and (c) they require one to validate your teaching ability.

Bunting (1997) advises that administrators may also use a beginning teacher's portfolio as a part of the initial screening process, to prioritize applicants who appear equally qualified, and to use as a baseline for ongoing professional growth.

Boody and Montecinos (1997) emphasize the advantages of administrative use of portfolios as "direct evidence of actual classroom performance" and "a concrete basis for insightful screening and interviewing" (p. 34).

Although some applicants will obtain a job without a portfolio, others believe that portfolios are becoming vital instruments in securing employment. As one colleague stated in an e-mail message, "If a student comes in without a portfolio, you wonder about them." Regardless of requirements, interview committees will be impressed with a well-organized professional portfolio. Because research indicates that a portfolio is most likely to be requested during a follow-up interview with the building principal, finalists need something to separate them from the rest of the pack. A portfolio affords that advantage.

Summary

Once the portfolio is compiled, the final step of presenting the portfolio is crucial. The successful applicant (whether applying for that first job or applying for tenure) must be prepared for the interview, display outstanding interpersonal skills, dress appropriately, ask questions, and be able to problem-solve and articulate skillfully. Familiarizing oneself with the process and knowing how to use the portfolio adeptly will relay an air of confidence and preparedness to the interviewer.

Questions

1. What are some desirable behaviors that may be demonstrated in an interview?

2. Should one ever refuse to answer a question during an interview? If so, when?

3. Do you think it helps or hurts the interviewee to ask questions?

4. How can one practice for an interview?

Topics for Consideration

1. Design a checklist of things to do before and after an interview.

2. Compile a list of questions that you might ask during an interview.

3. Review your resume and update as needed. Decide whether the resume reflects your current skills. If not, create an action plan that would "fill in the gaps" of weak areas.

4. Using the Frequently Asked Questions included in this chapter, partner with another person and do a mock interview. Have a third person rate you on the quality of your questions (see Resource G).

9

Electronic Portfolios

Kendyl wanted to become a teacher. She had completed her general education requirements and was now ready to learn how to teach. She was surprised when her adviser told her that she must enroll in Portfolio 101 and that she would be required to create an "electronic portfolio" that could be accessed online or be saved to a CD.

In addition to creating the portfolio, she would be expected to update the portfolio over the next two years, to fulfill the university's competency requirements. Dr. Capps told her that, when completed, the portfolio would include videos of her student teaching and have several types of multimedia incorporated into the design.

It made her nervous to know that her teaching skills would be on display for future employers and that digital video and photos would be used to confirm her ability to create, teach, and evaluate a unit of study for students. Somehow all this use of technology was different from what she thought it would be. It is one thing to tell an employer that you have the skills to teach and quite another to actually demonstrate those skills by providing digital images, scanned documents, and video.

While Kendyl felt comfortable using the computer for word processing and using the Internet and e-mail, she didn't know much about digital technology or how to operate the equipment needed to pull all the required components together. Now she not only was concerned about what to include in the portfolio, but also about the time it would take to learn the skills, electronically compile the information, and put together a professional presentation.

In the boardroom and the classroom, no matter what the age or the grade, people in the twenty-first century are finding that regardless how much one resists or rages or gripes, technology is here to stay. Carson is discovering it in his mom's lap. Kendyl is learning the fact while completing her Bachelor's degree, and in the meantime, Grandpa Buster is checking out his AARP benefits online. E-mail addresses are exchanged a million times daily and are a necessary item on business cards. So, get over it, and let's determine just how technology can help us and specifically, what it has to do with portfolio development.

What's All the Fuss?

Why are so many schools, companies, and universities turning to the electronic portfolio? There are several reasons, but one of the most compelling is the fact that many national organizations are now advocating the use of portfolios. Electronic portfolios are used not only to support individual student teacher assessment and document growth, but also as a means to market educational institutions. The institutional portfolio has become the latest in a series of national bandwagon strategies to restore confidence and provide greater community access to educational institutions.

> *Today's teacher candidates will teach tomorrow as they are taught today.*
>
> (NCATE, 1997)

Educational Standards

Tooting the technology horn, as long ago as 1993 the United States Department of Education included a document titled "Using Technology to Support Education Reform" in the U.S. Education Reform Studies. To summarize, the study reviewed ways that technology and reform agendas could complement one another, particularly in the support of constructivist forms of authentic and active learning.

They discovered that technology can support the assessment of student work in various ways and is also useful for guiding instruction. Specifically, technology facilitates (1) obtaining a trace of student thinking processes, (2) collecting real-time feedback from multiple students, (3) storing and retrieving student work-associated comments, and (4) setting individual goals and managing instruction (U.S. Department of Education, 1993).

In 1997, the National Council for Accreditation of Teacher Education (NCATE) concluded that before college students will utilize technology as a teaching tool, they must first be able to understand and effectively implement technology skills themselves. Ah! What a revelation! Preservice teachers must be technologically literate themselves before that same technology will become integrated into the classrooms of our world.

The NCATE task force stated that "today's teacher candidates will teach tomorrow as they are taught today." They recommended that teacher education programs should provide early experiences (electronic portfolio development?) for their students so that technology will be integrated into other education reform efforts. Not just focusing on the use of technology as a tool for performance assessment of teacher candidates, but truly meshing technology into their everyday life as students, and eventually as teachers (see Resource H).

More recently, the National Board for Professional Teaching Standards (NBPTS) (see Chapter 10), working in conjunction with the International Society for Technology in Education (ISTE), has created technology performance indicators for students as young as pre-kindergarten. Huge amounts of money have been poured into common and higher educational coffers to create, expand, and enhance technology programs. Teachers and students are expected to meet the standards that will ensure a technologically savvy workforce. It is only logical that the same standards be applied to those who are becoming teachers.

So, if we are to tame the technology tiger, we must have some basic understanding of what the "beast" actually is. What are its strengths? Where is it vulnerable? Then, how can we use the "animal" to our advantage?

> *Having a basic literacy that incorporates technological knowledge/skill and self-reliance requires that learners are able to demonstrate their knowledge and abilities rather than conform to prescribed evaluation procedures. Demonstration of knowledge and ability requires a platform capable of capturing, storing, displaying, and transmitting this ability. We have entered a new world, a portfolio world.*
>
> (Bergman, 2003)

What Is an Electronic Portfolio?

Would a rose by any other name smell as sweet? Whether we call them Web folios, digital folios, cyber-portfolios or electronic portfolios, we are still referring to student portfolios made available on a CD or the Internet. Yet as the portfolio has evolved from pencil and paper (or word processor and paper), so has its definition.

The portfolio is no longer just an assessment tool, but rather is an organic student-centered instructional tool that progressively and deliberately documents student growth and integrates all facets of a student's learning experiences, those inside and outside the school walls.

Electronic portfolios are selective and purposeful collections of student work made available on the WWW. Portfolios focus on the students' reflections on their own works. They are records of learning, growth, and change. They provide meaningful documentation of students' abilities. Electronic portfolios provide information to students, parents, teachers and members of the community about what students have learned or are able to do. They represent a learning history. (Ash, 2003)

At Albion College Department of Education (2003), a twenty-first century definition has emerged:

> A digital portfolio is self-guiding, meaning that the author uses computer software to structure the presentation so that a reader can easily navigate and understand what is present. For example, you may construct a Web-based portfolio and assume that the reader knows how to traverse from page to page via links. More importantly, always provide the reader with a sense of where he or she "is" at any given time—why the information on a page is important, where they can choose to go next, and how to access ancillary documents. The portfolio is also self-contained, so that all the hardware and software that the reader needs to install and view the portfolio is clearly defined and/or included on the media. Most importantly, it integrates text, graphics, video, audio and other formats to accurately convey the big picture, a portrait of the person as a teacher.

How It's the Same as a Paper Portfolio

Certain characteristics are essential to the development of any type of portfolio. According to Barton and Collins (1997), portfolios should be

- Multi-sourced (include both people and artifacts)
- Authentic (context and evidence are directly linked)
- Dynamic (capturing growth and change)
- Explicit (purpose and goals are clearly defined)
- Integrated (evidence should establish a correspondence between program activities and life experiences)
- Based on ownership (the participant helps determine evidence to include and goals to be met)
- Multi-task assessments (simultaneously assess program effectiveness and individual performance)

How It's Different from a Paper Portfolio

Electronic portfolios provide wider dimensions of learning that just paper-and-pencil reports of exercises. For example, in an electronic portfolio a student can play a digitized tape of the most important part of his lesson or show a movie or PowerPoint demonstration of how he was able to expand a lesson using the Internet.

The entire portfolio can be interconnected through hyperlinks. Papers and materials do not get lost or misplaced. New student work can replace older work with minimal effort. Electronic portfolios save space and can be stored on a school's network or even on an external disk such as the Zip cartridge. They can then be transported to another school with ease. (Tuttle, 1997)

Advantages of Electronic Portfolios

There are many documented advantages to using electronic portfolios. Niguidula (1993) states that the goal of digital portfolios is not to demonstrate technology but to show more effectively what students are capable of doing in a content area, and bring a school's vision and standards to life by having the students take ownership of their work (p. 8).

Advantages:

- Fosters active learning
- Motivates students
- Is an instrument of feedback and provides an ongoing basis for discussion of student performance
- Demonstrates students' computer and technological literacy
- Results in an engaging and interactive presentation of skills
- Makes it easy to transmit, access, and store bulky items and large amounts of information
- Exhibits "benchmark" performances
- Is easy to upgrade and edit, providing an ongoing and current record of growth
- Organizes and presents personal reflections and course assignments in various forms, such as graphics, text, sound files, and video
- Allows cross-referencing of student work
- Directly relates student work to specific standards
- Makes work portable, accessible, and more easily and widely distributed
- Is comprehensive without being cumbersome
- Provides students with an opportunity to "explore, extend, showcase, and reflect on their own learning" (Dietz, 1995, p. 40)
- Encourages diverse and numerous possibilities for integrating assessment into the daily life of the classroom
- Supports constructivist forms of authentic and active learning by preserving and presenting learners' progress, benchmarks, and goals
- Has the potential to enhance the education of teacher candidates and prepare them to use computer technology in their classrooms
- Proves to prospective employers technical skills and independent learning and creativity
- Is extremely durable and lasts indefinitely

Electronic portfolios provide a nurturing environment for novice preservice teachers by serving as a bridge between theory and practice while providing an opportunity to develop as a reflective practitioner through effective clinical supervision and coaching. Electronic portfolios are rare connectors that can and should provide actual linkage between theory and practice. Mentors, through the use of documents and multimedia, now lead preservice teachers to develop internal dialogue that supports effective teaching. Waiting to schedule bi-semester evaluation conferences is now archaic. With our technological advances, a mentor teacher can provide immediate feedback for beginning teachers, demonstrating through real-time instruction. The novice teacher can then use the tapes to validate professional growth (Boulware, Bratina, Holt, & Johnson, 1997).

Disadvantages of Electronic Portfolios

There are naysayers that will discourage any new educational idea by focusing only on the negative aspects. As with any new assessment tool, portfolios, and especially electronic ones, have their fair share of critics. Knowing some of the limitations and possible problems with electronic portfolios will help avoid the inevitable potholes on the road to successful implementation and showcasing of the product.

Disadvantages:

- Ensuring availability and accessibility of hardware and software used to capture and store portfolios
- Inability of some individuals and institutions to provide adequate disk storage and backup capabilities
- Labor-intensive and time-consuming aspects of planning, compiling, and administering
- Difficult to establish commonalities due to the diverse nature of participants and different focuses and uses
- Lack of strong commitment and understanding from university and common school administrators to teachers to students
- Concern regarding ways to ensure security and password protection
- Confusing for those with limited understanding of the process and futile without the support and direction of knowledgeable mentors
- May be seen as less reliable or fair than more quantitative evaluations such as test scores
- Like other qualitative data, information included in the portfolio can be difficult to analyze or aggregate to show change
- Not as useful in allowing one to rank participants or programs, including comparisons of norms, in a quantitative or standardized way. Although portfolios can (and often do) include some standardized test scores along with other kinds of evidence, this is not the main purpose of the portfolio (Sewell, Marczak, & Horn, 1997)

> *Electronic portfolio development is like a gas: it will occupy any volume it is provided.*
>
> (Borden & Thomas, 2001)

What to Consider When Planning an Electronic Portfolio

Creating an electronic portfolio is not unlike directing a huge production. Before attempting to develop a digital portfolio, one needs to think about the direction and ultimate goal of the portfolio. As with paper portfolios, the CORP process can be followed. The developer must Collect, Organize, Reflect, and Present. The primary difference lies in the manner of collection and presentation.

While accumulating artifacts, it is important to know whether one will be creating a paper or electronic portfolio. If one is unsure which type of portfolio will be designed, then it is best to collect information and artifacts as if it were an electronic portfolio. While it is possible to create an electronic portfolio from a paper one, doing so may forfeit the richness that would be available if one included photographs, interactive video, and audio. The type of artifacts one collects will ultimately determine the type of portfolio that can be preserved and presented.

Another early consideration is where to store the electronic media—on a compact disk, the college server, or a password-protected Web site. It's vital to choose a location that will allow easy access, ensure safety and confidentiality of records and documents, and yet still be flexible enough to allow updating of information.

Five Questions to Ask

Helen Barrett (1998) believes the following five questions should be asked prior to creating an electronic portfolio:

1. What is the purpose of the portfolio?
   Determining the audience will determine the purpose of the portfolio. Possible audiences include teachers, students, administrators, parents, communities, and employers, with each of them desiring a specific result from the portfolio viewing.

2. How will you store the working portfolio?
   You must decide where the draft portfolio will be kept. The location should provide easy access and reliable storage. Possibilities include rewriteable compact disks, videotape, high-density disks, papers that can be scanned, intranets, or password-protected servers.

3. How will you publish the formal portfolio?
   The formal or presentation portfolio may require a different publication format. Keep in mind your audience and determine what technology will be available to those viewing your finished product. Will a CD-ROM work best or perhaps a Web page where they can find the necessary documents?

4. How will you guarantee secure assessment information?
   Ensuring that your electronically stored information remains confidential is critical. What precautions will you take to keep it secure?

5. Can you use technology to collect observational assessment data?
   Two programs are available for collecting data—Learner Profile and Grady Profile. Grady Profile is the only program capable of storing portfolio items. These are for wide-scale assessment data; individual data can be documented with relative ease.

Additional Assessment Factors

When creating an electronic portfolio, keep in mind how much time is available before the portfolio is presented, what standards and outcomes will be addressed, and what multimedia formats will be included.

Many people want to include all the "bells and whistles" in an electronic portfolio, but forget that they still don't know how to program their VCR. If you aren't already skilled in multimedia presentations, consider the time it will take to learn how to create the portfolio. The Rubric for Assessing Electronic Portfolios (Resource I) addresses specific components of electronic portfolio development, and provides guidance for creating an electronic portfolio.

Creating an electronic portfolio can develop teachers' as well as students' multimedia technology skills, but can seem daunting. What is gained is a powerful tool for demonstrating professional growth over time. The multimedia development process usually covers the following stages:

- Assess/Decide. Assess the needs of the audience, the presentation goals, and the appropriate tools for the final portfolio presentation.
- Design/Plan. Focus on organizing and designing the presentation. Determine audience-appropriate content, software, storage medium, and presentation sequence. Construct flow charts and write storyboards.
- Develop. Gather materials to include in the presentation and organize them into a sequence (or use hyperlinks) for the best presentation of the material, using an appropriate multimedia authoring program.
- Implement. Present the portfolio to the intended audience.
- Evaluate. Focus on evaluating the presentation's effectiveness in light of its purpose.

Hardware

The basic hardware to develop an electronic portfolio is readily available in most universities. Computers, printers, scanners, digital cameras (for moving and still pictures), CD-ROM and Zip drives, and so forth are found on college campuses all over the world. Although the hardware may be available, decisions still must be made about which programs to use to create the portfolio.

Software

Images, sound, and video certainly can enrich and expand the portfolio's possibilities, and there are many good programs that are easy to learn.

Educational divisions of software companies have expanded exponentially and are delighted to provide various programs to students and teachers looking for ways to create digital portfolios easily and quickly. Additionally, some universities have created their own CD-ROMs to assist preservice teachers with the preparation of professional portfolios. The CD-ROM Project at the University of North Florida's College of Education and Human Services was developed "to assist preservice teachers in the preparation of their professional portfolios as tools for reflection and to evaluate the skills and knowledge attained during their two semesters of clinical education" (Boulware, 1998). User-friendly tools become paramount as many educators are still seeking a toehold to master our ever-changing technology.

The software mentioned in this chapter is primarily "off the shelf" and can be purchased from most office supply and computer stores. Software commonly used for portfolio development includes: FileMaker Pro, Grady Profile from Aurbach and Associates, Portfolio Assessment Toolkit, Movie Player Pro, Apple Video Player, iMovie, PowerPoint, ClarisWorks, Gold Disk's Astound, HyperStudio, Digital Chisel, Macromedia Authorware, Netscape Composer, Director, Claris Home Page, Toolbook, Superlink, Adobe Acrobat Exchange, Microsoft Office Works and FrontPage, and AppleWorks.

These programs vary in ease of use, hardware requirements, cost, and appropriateness for different audiences. For a comprehensive list of the software, Web sites, and contact information, see Resource J.

Levels of Technological Sophistication

The student developing an electronic portfolio generally follows a path from least technologically savvy to most sophisticated, with many plateaus in between. Helen Barrett's (2000) article "Create Your Own Electronic Portfolio" rates the levels of sophistication from 0 to 5. These levels should be considered when determining the depth of digital waters in which one is willing to swim.

- Level 0: the compiler has all documents in paper format, with perhaps some stored on videotape.

- Level 1: documents have been created using a word processor and are stored on a computer hard drive, diskette, or LAN server.
- Level 2: data is further structured in a database or HyperStudio template, or in a slide show such as PowerPoint or AppleWorks, and stored as before or on a Zip drive.
- Level 3: documents are translated into Portable Document Format (PDF) with hyperlinks between standards and artifacts, and stored as before or on a CD-RW.
- Level 4: documents are translated into HTML with accompanying hyperlinks using a Web authoring program, and posted as a Web page on an Internet server.
- Level 5: the portfolio is organized with a multimedia-authoring program, incorporating both sound and video that has been converted to a digital format and saved on a CD-RW or posted to the Internet in streaming format.

So whether one chooses simply to wade the waters of electronic portfolio development or dive deeply, there is a place for everyone.

Organizations Promoting Electronic Portfolios

> *Teachers need an "attitude" that is fearless in the use of technology, encourages them to take risks, and inspires them to become lifelong learners.*
>
> (NCATE, 1997)

The push is on. Accountability is in. Technology is in. Standards are in. Spending on technology for K–12 education has climbed steadily, exceeding $5 billion annually by some estimates. All 50 states have plans in place for educational technology and are steadily appropriating money for those plans. Thirty-eight states have technology requirements for teaching candidates or teacher preparation programs (Robelen, 1999).

What is driving the technology push? For one thing, international, national, and state standards are mandating that teachers be knowledgeable in the use of technology. They are expected to know not only how to use the various tools, but how to integrate those skills and implement technology in the classrooms. It makes perfect sense, then, that being able to master electronic skills is a vital piece in a teacher's repertoire. Producing an electronic portfolio is one area in which teachers and prospective teachers can demonstrate what they know.

NCATE standards expect the use of technology to be vital to teacher preparation during the twenty-first century and beyond.

Uses of technology for instruction and assessment have been recognized as a vital component of teacher preparation in the standards.

NCATE expects that the education unit's conceptual framework include a commitment to preparing candidates who are able to use educational technology to help all students learn. (NCATE, 2003)

ISTE has outlined six areas with performance indicators designed for preservice and veteran teachers. Teachers should be able to (1) demonstrate a sound understanding of technology operations and concepts, (2) plan and design effective learning environments and experiences supported by technology, (3) implement curriculum plans that include methods and strategies for applying technology to maximize student learning, (4) apply technology to facilitate a variety of effective assessment and evaluation strategies, (5) use technology to enhance their productivity and professional practice, and (6) understand the social, ethical, legal, and human issues surrounding the use of technology in PreK–12 schools and apply those principles in practice (ISTE, n.d.).

NBPTS requires that candidates seeking National Board Certification develop a portfolio that meets exacting guidelines, including the use of technology (see Chapter 10).

Using Electronic Portfolios in the Job Search

One of the primary uses of an electronic portfolio is to show one's skills to a prospective employer. From handing an administrator a custom-made CD to posting a page on the Internet, students are seeking an edge in a competitive job market.

An advantage of a cyber-portfolio (one that is posted on a Web site) is that future employers can access the portfolio anytime and anyplace. Producing a polished presentation with extensive multimedia content, while incorporating standards and pertinent resume and personal information, can have an immediate and positive impact on employability.

In a recently syndicated "Job Talk" column, Joyce Laine Kennedy (1995) observes that employers are hiring people who know what performance is all about, who know that doing a job is more important than holding one.

> Using a portfolio in the search for work helps put the job seeker in tune with the new emphasis on *portability*. Constructing a portfolio requires looking upon a career as a collection of experiences, which can be grouped and re-ordered to match the changing direction of one's career journey.

Looking at examples of portfolios and seeing the possibilities for personal growth, tenure advancement, job opportunities, and ongoing personal and professional development aids in discovering the route one would like to take when creating one's own online portfolio.

Regardless of the choice of media for your portfolio, remember to select a format that not only suits your personality but also one that highlights your own personal strengths. For more information regarding portfolios and employment, see Chapter 8 and Resource C.

Summary

Electronic portfolios are becoming more and more popular. Educators who can demonstrate they have the skills not only to utilize technology for their own personal use, but to incorporate it into their classroom teaching, assessment, professional development, and career searches will have a distinct advantage. A teacher's experiences will evolve through his or her career, and by using a variety of multimedia to spotlight those ever-improving skills and abilities, he or she will be able to demonstrate that growth and provide an ongoing "diary" of professional development. Being able to document a lifetime of experiences that, quite literally, can be held in the palm of a hand, is nothing short of miraculous.

Questions

1. How is technology changing the way in which we communicate and document experiences?

2. Name five advantages and five disadvantages of electronic portfolios.

3. How are electronic portfolios like and unlike paper portfolios?

4. Explain how a hyperlink would be used in an electronic portfolio.

5. What privacy issues are involved in creating a Web folio?

Topics for Consideration

1. Examine the following portfolios online and discuss what you liked and did not like about them.
   Kathleen Fischer's Portfolio: www.durak.org/kathy/portfolio/index. html
   Carolyn F. Austin: www.ags.uci.edu/~cfaustin/
   Joseph A. Braun, Jr., An Electronic Teaching Portfolio: www.coe.ilstu. edu/jabraun/braun/professional.html

2. Use the Self-Evaluation Rubrics for Basic Teacher Computer Use in Resource H to determine your own level of technology skills. Discuss where you need to improve or skills you would like to learn.

3. Explain the quote "Electronic portfolio development is like a gas: it will occupy any volume it is provided" (Borden & Thomas, 2001).

4. Discuss which you think is best, electronic or paper portfolios. Defend your answer with facts.

10

Portfolios for National Board Certification

Two teachers who had several years of experience talked during their planning period as they enjoyed a cup of coffee in the faculty lounge of their building. Alice had been an English teacher for four years, and according to her evaluations by her principal and the students, she was an excellent teacher. Todd, her colleague in the lounge, had been an algebra teacher for six years.

"Ever thought of getting the National Board Certification so that you could get that extra $50,000 over the next few years?" Todd asked.

"As a matter of fact, I am in the process of doing that very thing. What about you?" Alice responded.

"I would try for it, but I am just afraid of that portfolio that's required. I don't know whether or not I could ever get that done. I've heard that it is such a job, and so much depends on how well it is done."

"It is a time-consuming process, but a task that can be conquered," Alice told him. "I have a plan that I am working through now. It's a process called CORP: collection of good artifacts about my teaching career, organization of the materials in a specific sequence, reflection on each of the artifacts that I have chosen, and a proper presentation of those ideas in a way that catches the reader's attention," she told him.

"When you explain the process in that way, it doesn't seem nearly so formidable. That $50,000 the state promised after we complete the National Board Certification is certainly appealing, with all the economic changes in this world we live in. I don't know anyone who couldn't stand to have a few thousand extra each year," Todd concluded.

National Board for Professional Teaching Standards (NBPTS) Certification has become a challenge for many teachers who qualify for that recognition. Having the certification gives teachers a feeling of satisfaction, knowing that they are among the elite of the national teaching force. In most states, financial rewards add to the benefits for those who hold the certification. Attaining NBPTS Certification is a rigorous process, but those who have persevered and achieved the goal, even if they do not receive extra pay, greatly enhance their self-esteem. The number of teachers attaining the certification grows each year, but certified teachers are still a very small percentage of the vast number of teachers across the nation.

How Is a Portfolio Part of the NBPTS Certification Process?

The NBPTS assessment has two phases, one of which is the preparation of a portfolio that represents the candidate's professional life. The Board prescribes exactly the materials the portfolio must contain. One can still individualize it with reflections on items included within the NBPTS requirements. For this portfolio, however, the reflections are called "written commentary." The portfolio is a large part of the historical documentation that is required for the assessment of the candidate. The other part involves demonstrating how the candidate works with instructional materials and how the candidate evaluates the materials that he or she teaches in the classroom. There are several kinds of artifacts that can be included in a collection of materials. Videotapes of the candidate teaching, samples of students' works, and exhibits of work they have done in their classrooms and other places all help to make up the list of items that they will reflect upon in their portfolios. The candidates tie their artifacts to the standards of their disciplines with strands representative of their field. All of the standards and the strands must link directly to the NBPTS core propositions.

How Do I Establish Parameters for This Portfolio?

Though assembling this specialized showcase portfolio is a great opportunity for the teacher, the process is not so different from that used by beginning teachers to document their ability to meet state competency mandates. The NBPTS Certification portfolio, though much more comprehensive, represents the same kind of documentation. The object of the portfolio is still to tell the story of the candidate's teaching career. The compiler is required to collect artifacts that flesh out the bare bones of his or her story. The collection is designed to highlight that candidate's skill in the classroom.

Just as student teachers or beginning teachers draw on resources such as the Internet or professorial notes for lesson plan samples to include in their portfolios, the NBPTS Certification candidate may rely on materials that he or she has prepared to meet the prescribed NBPTS standards and the strands. The candidates must establish that they can follow certain learning strands, and in so doing, prove that they are exemplary teachers. Each teacher preparing any kind of portfolio must work under the pressure of special deadlines. All artifacts, whether of the beginning teacher or master teacher, must meet certain collection parameters. The parameters will ensure that the showcase portfolio is not just a compendium of pictures or a scrapbook of life works, but a collection of items that represent best works and fulfill the purpose of the portfolio.

Collecting artifactual materials for the NBPTS Certification showcase portfolio will result in an overwhelming amount of data to review. All who seek certification are master teachers with mounds of artifacts to verify their work. The candidates must remember to organize these artifacts to best show their works. While collecting artifacts, candidates must think about how they will reflect on the material, so that anyone who sees their collection will understand the value of that work in relation to their teaching careers.

The materials that are included in any portfolio should demonstrate how an excellent teacher actually teaches. The collection of artifacts should not be artificially created for the purpose of the portfolio, but should come from the materials the teachers naturally use within their learning strands to meet the standards set for their disciplines. Of course, some plans may have to be expanded to make their usage more universal or more practical, to fit the prescribed standards. However, plans should always reflect what the candidates commonly do in their own classrooms. The whole process is designed to get a representative sampling of the candidates' works, so that evaluators will know, without a doubt, that the candidates are worthy of the national recognition that goes with the NBPTS Certification. The overlying question is, "Does the collection of artifacts in the portfolio reflect how well the candidate's classroom practices capture the national standards and fulfill the strands set for the field in which that candidate teaches?"

How Does the Portfolio Complement the NBPTS Core Propositions?

The five core propositions used by the NBPTS are as follows:

1. Teachers are committed to students and their learning.

2. Teachers know the subjects they teach and how to teach those subjects to students.

3. Teachers are responsible for managing and monitoring student learning.

4. Teachers think systematically about their practice and learn from experience.

5. Teachers are members of learning communities.

These core propositions describe the knowledge, skills, and dispositions that a quality teacher must achieve. They are the standards that must be demonstrated in undergraduate and graduate student portfolios, to show that the students will become exemplary teachers. The standards are rapidly working their way into all educational assessment portfolios.

Teachers who plan to become NBPTS Certified teachers first have to choose the area in which they wish to be certified. They then request the certification package. This in itself is a challenging process; one can find information about it on the Internet (see Resource C). The process involves a significant investment of both money and time. Contact your state Department of Education to find out whether financial aid is available, and whether certified teachers in your state receive additional remuneration or other advantages.

The plan of the NBPTS is to begin with the core proposition that the student is foremost in the educational process. Once the core proposition is ingrained, the candidate must choose a strand of learning to be the focus of his or her work. The candidate, using that chosen strand, examines the areas of competency for the strand within the standards set by the discipline in which they teach. The teachers gather work samples from the students. The work may be poor, fair, good, excellent, or superior—the reflection on these samples is not examining the work but the way the teacher relates the materials to the standards and the learning strands. Next, the teacher designs action plans to tie the work to the program's core propositions. For instance, in a language arts NBPTS Certification process, teachers select the area in which they teach. They might choose young adults or they might choose early adolescent language arts. The teachers then isolate the standards of reading, writing, speaking, listening, and viewing, then organize their teaching plans so that they correspond to the strands of audience, purpose, and the vernacular. These lesson plans and the documentation from the assignments they have collected are then attached to those standards and strands so that they can relate back into the core propositions. Those who can tie these items together and actually meet the needs created in their plans can then produce pertinent artifacts. These artifacts, the students' works, will show that the teacher is able to tie into the processes set by the strands, standards, and core propositions. The candidates can then reflect with a written commentary, showing why those particular artifacts should be used in their portfolios as examples of the teachers' best works.

How Do Subject Area Standards Help with Planning the Portfolio?

Once the area of certification is chosen and the package from the NBPTS has been received, the candidate needs to study the standards that are set for the certificate area chosen. The package gives very detailed methods for studying the standards and meeting the standards through the learning strands as the candidate works on the portfolio. Another valuable part of the package is a school year time line, with the application scheduled early in the first semester and the deadline near the end of the second semester. There is also a specific glossary of terms used when discussing the portfolio, its artifacts, and its commentaries. The NBPTS guidelines suggest that the candidate encourage colleagues to help with the tasks of filming, critiquing of the videotape, reading the portfolio for specific strand-oriented content, and then finally, proofreading for typographical errors. All of these aids are very important because of the specificity of materials prescribed for the NBPTS showcase portfolio. The same process is followed when one uses CORP to build a showcase portfolio, but in much greater and more prescribed detail.

What Is the Challenge of Collecting Data for the NBPTS Portfolio?

One of the most important challenges of the NBPTS portfolio is the collecting process. Choose the artifacts for your showcase portfolio that will best show your teaching capability. The student work samples you select must be the right artifacts to demonstrate the relationships and specialized associations that the master teacher has to accomplish to hold National Certification. The collection should confirm that the teacher has a plan of action to bring students to the appropriate level of competence. Teachers will want to choose artifacts that best display their teaching, and that they can most effectively justify in writing as the third step in a good portfolio, the reflection or written commentary.

Student work samples are the artifacts that may best show the abilities of a teacher in a showcase portfolio. This idea has expanded so rapidly in recent months that now student work samples seem the most accurate way of evaluating a teacher's capability. Student work samples have become significant for assessing how college and university education departments meet the standards set by nationally recognized learned societies. Each society has its own standards. Many education departments have started to demand work samples to substantiate that they are meeting the learned societies' standards. Universities once were allowed to submit syllabi to show that individual courses they offered adhered to their learned society's standards. These courses met the standards through classroom instruction. Now, many of the societies demand samples gathered from the students the candidate teachers teach, as an integral part of program reviews and accreditation packages. The samples will prove the standards are met, so syllabi are no longer accepted as proof of accomplishment. If the professor does not complete the syllabus, the work samples you collect will become more and more valuable for your assessment as time passes. The greatest achievement for a teacher is to see your students perform according to a universally accepted standard, and see that the learning strands for that standard are followed. The idea of just meeting a teacher's plan, or teaching to parents' or student's satisfaction, will no longer suffice as proof of accomplishment. The work samples provide forceful evidence that the teacher can meet the core propositions set by the NBPTS.

The artifacts (work samples) are evidence that the teacher has reached educational goals for the grade level taught. If the artifact that you collect for your portfolio has multiple interpretations, that particular artifact would probably not be suitable for the showcase portfolio. The evaluator should see on first reading that the documentation proves the teacher's capability. Reflections on the artifacts, in this case the student work samples, must indicate how and what the students learned as a result of the way the students were taught by the candidate.

Keep in mind that the candidate using student work samples must have written permission of the students involved, and the parents or guardians of those students who are minors, to use the materials for display.

How Is the CORP Process Used in NBPTS Portfolios?

That which CORP suggests as organization and presentation are relatively easy to accomplish within the NBPTS guidelines. The NBPTS plan is very prescriptive; the proposed presentation of the material is outlined in the guidebook. Collecting and organizing individual artifacts is within the candidate's discretion. The candidate still may select specific student work samples to best show his or her teaching. The candidate then may follow the prescribed overall organization for the portfolio. There are specific outlines and guidelines to follow for each of the standards within the discipline in which one teaches. There are page limits for describing activities, and there are page limits for reflections on that activity and that sample. One may not vary the presentation from the prescribed plan set forth by NBPTS. This presentation will require very special planning, but once that is done, following the CORP process will help to make the presentation reflect the guidelines. Once the candidate has received the guidelines package, it is a good idea to check them off, rubric style, as each is explicitly followed. If that is done, one can feel confident that the presentation in on target.

Similarities Between
"Reflection" and "Written Commentary"

The reflective stage (the R of CORP) may follow several different avenues including true reflection (see Chapter 4), descriptions of process, and analyses of the activities. These are stated explicitly in the guidelines for the NBPTS Certification. They must be adhered to without variation, but a reflection is a reflection, and the guidelines earlier in this volume should still aid one in composing the written commentary for the NBPTS portfolio. Explanations required as written commentary may not fit the exact guidelines we stated about reflections, but they are nonetheless reflections, even if they are extremely specialized. One may be asked to analyze the process used to characterize the artifact or students' work processes so that evaluators can understand them. Written commentary could take on any or all of the attributes which we refer to as reflection. Reflection generally explains how the artifactual process affects the understanding of one's disposition, knowledge, or skill on a given subject. A rubric we suggest for writing reflections asks the writer to tell something of the "how" and "why" of the process so that he or she may best show the skills, knowledge, and disposition generated by the specific artifact used. Perhaps this differs slightly from the NBPTS interpretation of reflection, and the compiler of the NBPTS portfolio must follow their guidelines. An important aspect of the reflection process, as well as the written commentary, is that the writing must be as objective and as accurate as possible so that the artifact and its reason for inclusion do not have to be interpreted by the reviewer. The teacher's purpose in presenting a well-prepared portfolio, whether applying for a job or NBPTS Certification, is to prove objectively that he or she is an excellent candidate to receive the desired recognition.

In fact, the NBPTS requirements are no more difficult than the requirements of a good professional portfolio. They are just slightly different in process. One has to know the theory and the vocabulary for each. One must follow the guidelines of each, although the NBPTS guidelines are much more specific. One must be objective in the production of the showcase portfolio. One must collect, organize, reflect upon, and present (CORP) the materials to the best possible advantage for the candidate. The more sophisticated the portfolio, the more work that may be required to present that portfolio well. A professional is a professional and must show a professional attitude whether in the NBPTS portfolio presentation or in a standard portfolio presentation of any kind.

A standard portfolio requires a time span of a year up to a lifetime of teaching to showcase one's career and competencies gained. One has to check the specific portfolio requirement with the assessor. If a portfolio is to be used for promotion or the establishment of tenure, as they sometimes are, then it must be carefully created and the artifacts in it must be appropriate to the goal of the portfolio. On the other hand, the generalized professional portfolio that is being used as a documentation for graduation or for a particular teaching job may be more holistic in its approach. The NBPTS allows some latitude for the candidate in selection of work samples for the portfolio, but the portfolio preparation is usually set to cover a school year. Candidates may exercise a great deal of discretion in the collection of the materials characterizing their teaching mode over that period of time.

Questions for Checking the Portfolio Format

Portfolio assessment is a good way to understand the professional who submits a portfolio. You may want to ask yourself, as you prepare your portfolio, whether it is prescriptive or holistic in its approach:

1. Does this portfolio show the best possible picture of me as an educator?

2. Does the portfolio reflect my knowledge of subject matter, my skills as a teacher, and my disposition as a practitioner in my specific field of teaching?

3. Does the portfolio meet the standards set by those who will judge the portfolio?

If the answer to any of the questions is not readily evident, then the compiler needs to work more on the portfolio. The portfolio needs to show that candidate's best work. Such a presentation may enable the candidate to gain the special recognition sought, gain the promotion, or receive tenure. The amount of effort expended in the preparation of the portfolio is proportional to the professional recognition that it can bring.

Summary

The NBPTS Certification requires a very detailed kind of portfolio with its own specific criteria for completion. The CORP process of collecting, organizing, reflecting, and presenting is still very important, even with a prescribed portfolio. Interpretation of the ideas varies slightly. Collecting refers to gathering student work samples at various times and in various situations for analysis, description, and reflection. The presentation of this specialized portfolio is very specific and prescriptive, but is not too different from any other portfolio presentation. The compiler is still responsible for making a presentation that will earn him or her the recognition sought. The organizational structure for NBPTS portfolios is also expressly prescribed, so that all the candidates applying for certification can be evaluated objectively. Page limits for reflections are prescribed and enforced. If one plans to apply for the NBPTS Certification, he or she will need to make the application very early in the school year, and will need to complete the process in about seven months. Portfolios must be submitted by a specified date.

Questions

1. How is the preparation for the NBPTS portfolio different from any other showcase portfolio preparation?

2. Where does one begin to prepare any specialized portfolio?

3. What is a "standard," and how does it affect a portfolio's preparation?

4. What is a student "work sample" and how is it meant to be used in this portfolio?

Topics for Consideration

1. Collect copies of three different students' work samples. Analyze in writing (in fewer than three pages) what is known from those papers about the student, about the topic being taught (its strand), about the standard being examined from your teaching discipline, and about your success as a teacher with the topic in the work samples.

2. Write a sample reflection of at least one page, but not more than two, on why the set of work samples you selected for Topic 1 are good samples to delineate your teaching mastery.

3. Assume that one of the work samples you chose above is not a good paper and doesn't accomplish that which you wanted to accomplish. Write a reflection of at least one page, and not more than two, on how you can justify keeping such a paper among the work samples in your portfolio.

4. Discuss in a group the best way of incorporating work samples, video-tapes, and other artifacts of your teaching into a portfolio in the form of a reflection.

Resources

Resource A

Descriptive Words to Enhance Education-Related Activities

Personal Traits

enthusiastic	optimistic	adaptable	flexible	energetic
diplomatic	courteous	sincere	honest	punctual
conscientious	methodical	reliable	supportive	friendly
poised	helpful	unselfish	polite	creative
reflective	persistent	motivated	independent	encouraging
patient	gentle	assertive	dependable	intelligent

Leadership Traits

organized	directed	collected	assembled	modeled
planned	arranged	advised	listened	surveyed
assessed	delivered	volunteered	corrected	reflected
provided	assisted	coordinated	created	drafted
assigned	protected	prepared	demonstrated	supervised
recruited	hosted	supported	trained	tutored

Lifelong Learning Traits

curious	eager	self-directed	innovative	excited
challenging	participating	learning	improving	developing
stimulating	motivated	analyzing	expressing	studying
assisting	changing	accepting	seeking	considering

Resource B

Oklahoma General Competencies for Teacher Licensure and Certification

(Adopted May 23, 1996, by the State Board of Education as required by Legislative House Bill 1549 for creation of a competency-based teacher preparation program to be implemented July 1, 1997.)

1. The teacher understands the central concepts and methods of inquiry of the subject matter discipline(s) he or she teaches and can create learning experiences that make these aspects of subject matter meaningful for students.

2. The teacher understands how students learn and develop, and can provide learning opportunities that support their intellectual, social, and physical development at all grade levels including early childhood, elementary, middle level, and secondary.

3. The teacher understands that students vary in their approaches to learning, and creates instructional opportunities that are adaptable to individual differences of learners.

4. The teacher understands curriculum integration processes and uses a variety of instructional strategies to encourage students' development of critical thinking, problem solving, performance skills, and effective use of technology.

5. The teacher uses best practices related to motivation and behavior to create learning environments that encourage positive social interaction, self-motivation, and active engagement in learning, thus providing opportunities for success.

6. The teacher develops knowledge of and uses communication techniques to foster active inquiry, collaboration, and supportive interaction in the classroom.

7. The teacher plans instruction based on curriculum goals, knowledge of the teaching/learning process, subject matter, students' abilities and differences, and the community, and adapts instruction based on assessment and reflection.

8. The teacher understands and uses a variety of assessment strategies to evaluate and modify the teaching/learning process ensuring the continuous intellectual, social, and physical development of the learner.

9. The teacher evaluates the effects of his or her choices and actions on others (students, parents, and other professionals in the learning community), modifies those actions when needed, and actively seeks opportunities for continued professional growth.

10. The teacher fosters positive interaction with school colleagues, parents/families, and organizations in the community to actively engage them in support of students' learning and well-being.

11. The teacher will have an understanding of the importance of assisting students with career awareness and the application of career concepts to the academic curriculum.

12. The teacher understands the process of continuous lifelong learning, the concept of making learning enjoyable, and the need for a willingness to change when the change leads to greater student learning and development.

13. The teacher understands the legal aspects of teaching including the rights of students and parents/families, as well as the legal rights and responsibilities of the teacher.

14. The teacher understands and is able to develop instructional strategies/plans based on the Oklahoma core curriculum.

15. The teacher understands the state teacher evaluation process, "Oklahoma Criteria for Effective Teaching Performance," and how to incorporate these criteria in designing instructional strategies.

Primary Source of Competencies

Competencies 1 through 10 are based on "Model Standards for Beginning Teacher Licensing and Development: A Resource for State Dialogue," prepared by the Council for Chief State School Officers' Interstate New Teacher Assessment and Support Consortium.

Competencies 11 through 13 were developed as a result of input from Oklahoma educators.

Competencies 14 and 15 are based on Oklahoma law.

Representation of development committee: elementary teachers including Teacher of the Year finalists, elementary principals, and professors of teacher education.

Sources: Information from the National Council for Accreditation of Teacher Education (NCATE), Elementary Education Task Force, and Oklahoma's Core Curriculum Pursuant to 70 0.5 11-106.6 § a.

Resource C

Online Resources for the Development of Teacher Portfolios

National Standards and Goals

- Association of Teacher Educators: Standards for Teacher Educators. Includes list of standards, indicators, evidence supporting proficiency, and assessment modes: www.ate1.org/teampublish/120_620_2171.cfm
- National Board for Professional Teaching Standards. Seeking National Board Certification, FAQs, Talk to Other Teachers, General Information, What Teachers Should Know and Be Able to Do: www.nbpts.org
- National Council for Accreditation of Teacher Education. Links to each coalition membership group including organizations representing teacher educators, teachers, policymakers, subject-specific areas, and others: www.ncate.org/standard/m_stds.htm
- President's and Secretary of Education's Priorities. All national initiatives and links to resources and documents. A must for educators: www.ed.gov/inits.html
- International Society for Technology in Education: www.iste.org

Portfolio Development

- American Association for Higher Education. Paper and electronic portfolio programs: www.aahe.org/teaching/pfoliosearch3.cfm
- Awesome Library: Teacher Portfolios. Provides information about types of portfolios, electronic portfolios, and guidelines for creating and using them: www.awesomelibrary.org/Office/Teacher/Assessment Information/ Portfolios.htm
- Dr. Helen Barrett's Bookmarks. Everything you need to know: transition.alaska.edu/www/portfolios/bookmarks.html
- The Kalamazoo Portfolio. Site designed for students to learn about it, create it, and use it. Contains a database of institutions using portfolios and sample portfolios: www.kzoo.edu/pfolio/index.html
- IUPUI Portfolio. From The Urban Universities Portfolio Project: www.imir.iupui.edu/portfolio/
- Resources: Budget and staff development for electronic portfolios. From Alaska, a bare-bones look at hardware, software, and other materials needed: www.uaa.alaska.edu/ed/portfolios/matrix.html

Electronic Portfolio Development

- AAHE Portfolio Clearinghouse: www.aahe.org/teaching/portfolio_db.htm
- Albion College Education Department: Digital Portfolio Project: www.albion.edu/education/fac_educ/dig_portfolio_resources.htm
- Alverno College's "Diagnostic Digital Portfolio Program": www.ddp.alverno.edu
- Analysis of a Curricular Transformation. Elizabeth Barkley's Home Page: kml2.carnegiefoundation.org/gallery/ebarkley/
- Barrett's Electronic Portfolios Homepage: www.electronicportfolios.com
- Carnegie Academy for the Scholarship of Teaching and Learning: www.carnegiefoundation.org/CASTL
- Creating and Using Portfolios on the Alphabet Superhighway: www.ash.udel.edu/ash/teacher/portfolio.html
- Digital Portfolios, Roger Williams University: www.rwu.edu/programs/sed/index.htm
- Electronic Portfolio Home Page: www.essdack.org/port/index.html
- Electronic Portfolios in Teacher Education: www.chapman.edu/soe/faculty/piper/EPWeb/
- Electronic Portfolios: Resources for Higher Education: aahe.ital.utexas.edu/electronicportfolios/index.html
- Preparing Tomorrow's Teachers to Use Technology: www.pt3.org/index.html
- Preservice Teacher Electronic Portfolio Handbook: www.rockhurst.edu/academic/education/portfolio.pdf
- Rubric for Assessing Electronic Portfolios by Joyce L. Morris: www.uvm.edu/~jmorris/rubricep.html
- Stanford University's Learning Lab "E-Folio": sll.stanford.edu/consulting/tools/efolio/
- Technology Checklist for Electronic Portfolios: www.tandl.vt.edu/TESH/tech_checklist.htm
- Technology in the Classroom: Electronic Portfolios in the K–12 Classroom: www.education-world.com/a_tech/tech111.shtml
- Washington State University Rising Junior Writing Portfolio Site: www.wsu.edu:8080/~bcondon/portpage.html

Sample Electronic Portfolios

- Center for Technology and Teacher Education (University of Virginia) Undergraduate and Graduate Portfolios: curry.edschool.virginia.edu/class/edlf/589-07/sample.html
- University of Florida Electronic Portfolios: www.coe.ufl.edu/school/PT3/Portfolios.html
- Kalamazoo College Portfolios: www.kzoo.edu/pfolio/

Resource D
Portfolio Planner

Student Name: Date:

Conferences Number:

Competency/standard (list one per sheet):

Evidence/documentation (include as many artifacts as required):

Artifact 1 (list):

    Theory/rationale/reflection:

    Application:

Artifact 2 (list):

    Theory/rationale/reflection:

    Application:

Other possible artifacts:

Artifacts to be obtained before next conference:

Resource E
Portfolio Quality Checklist

This is a checklist designed to assist students in producing a quality portfolio. Ask the following questions prior to portfolio submission:

1. Do the contents provide a clear summary of my experiences in the program and what was learned from them?

2. Do the contents provide a clear indication of my strengths as a prospective classroom teacher?

3. Do the contents indicate that I used classes, assignments, observations, and clinical experiences to think critically about the nature and purposes of schools and learning?

4. Do the contents provide a clear indication of my plans for continued professional development?

5. Do the artifacts include necessary integrated documentation of experiences?

6. Are written materials in the portfolio free from glaring errors in content and mechanics, including grammar, spelling, and punctuation?

7. Is the writing clear and well organized?

8. Are the contents well organized, neat, and professional as well as easy to use?

9. Does the portfolio clearly and thoroughly reflect my understanding of the competencies?

10. Do the contents reflect substantial evidence of critical assessment and selection of pertinent artifacts, with reflections revealing an insightful and thoughtful educator?

11. Are the materials appealing, lively, and appropriate, with proficiency demonstrated?

12. Are the reflective statements highly persuasive regarding the accomplishment of intended competency?

13. Do the personal accomplishments reflect a representation of me not seen in other artifacts? Do they include shared insights, important details, and a revelation of my thoughts?

Resource F
Rubric for Evaluating Portfolios

Name   Institution   Date

3 = Exceeds expectations   Competencies marked 0 are unsatisfactory and
2 = Meets expectations   require additional work. If one zero is given, a
1 = In progress   failing grade will be assigned. The assessor is
                                 encouraged to supplement this form with narrative
                                 comments.

Competencies

1. The teacher understands the central concepts and methods of   3 2   1   0
   inquiry of the subject matter discipline(s) he or she teaches,
   and can create learning experiences that make the subject
   matter meaningful for students.

2. The teacher understands how students learn and develop,   3 2   1   0
   and can provide learning opportunities that support their
   intellectual, social, and physical development at all grade
   levels including early childhood, elementary, middle, and
   secondary levels.

3. The teacher understands that students vary in their   3 2   1   0
   approaches to learning, and creates instructional opportunities that are adaptable to individual differences of learners.

4. The teacher understands curriculum integration processes   3 2   1   0
   and uses a variety of instructional strategies to encourage
   students' development of critical thinking, problem solving,
   performance skills, and effective use of technology.

5. The teacher uses best practices related to motivation and   3 2   1   0
   behavior to create learning environments that encourage positive social interaction, self-motivation, and active engagement in learning, thus providing opportunities for success.

6. The teacher develops a knowledge of and uses a variety of   3 2   1   0
   effective communication techniques to foster active inquiry,
   collaboration, and supportive interaction in the classroom.

7. The teacher plans instruction based on curriculum goals,   3 2   1   0
   knowledge of the teaching/learning process, subject matter,
   students' abilities and differences, and the community, and
   adapts instruction based on assessment and reflection.

8. The teacher understands and uses a variety of assessment   3   2   1   0
   strategies to evaluate and modify the teaching/learning
   process, ensuring the continuous intellectual, social, and
   physical development of the learner.

9. The teacher evaluates the effects of his/her choices and   3   2   1   0
   actions on others (students, parents, and other professionals in the learning community), modifies those
   actions when needed, and actively seeks opportunities
   for continued professional growth.

10. The teacher fosters positive interaction with school   3   2   1   0
    colleagues, parents/families, and organizations in the
    community to actively engage them in support of
    students' learning and well-being.

11. The teacher understands the importance of assisting   3   2   1   0
    students with career awareness and application of career
    concepts to the academic curriculum.

12. The teacher understands the process of continuous life-   3   2   1   0
    long learning, the concept of making learning enjoyable,
    and the need for a willingness to change when the change
    leads to greater student learning and development.

13. The teacher understands the legal aspects of teaching   3   2   1   0
    including the rights of students and parents/families and
    the legal rights and responsibilities of the teacher.

14. The teacher understands the core curriculum and is able   3   2   1   0
    to develop instructional strategies/plans based on state
    and national standards.

15. The teacher understands the state teacher evaluation   3   2   1   0
    process and knows how to incorporate those requirements
    when designing instructional strategies.

Pass _____   Fail _____   Reevaluate _____

Evaluator's Signature _____

Comments:

Resource G
Evaluation Rating Form for Interview

Interviewee Name: _____

Scholarship	Unsatisfactory	1	2	3	4	5	Excellent
Appearance	Poor	1	2	3	4	5	Superior
Personality	Insecure	1	2	3	4	5	Poised
Educational Philosophy	Diffused	1	2	3	4	5	Clear
Disposition	Negative/ Pessimist	1	2	3	4	5	Cheerful/ Positive
Knowledge of Basic Instruction	Unsatisfactory	1	2	3	4	5	Knowledgeable
Techniques of Classroom Management	Unsure	1	2	3	4	5	Fully Understood
Works Well With Parents	Uncooperative	1	2	3	4	5	Fully Able & Willing
References	Poor	1	2	3	4	5	Outstanding
Answers to Questions	Indirect	1	2	3	4	5	Direct
Questions Asked by Applicant	Unimportant	1	2	3	4	5	Important
Recommendation	Do Not Consider	1	2	3	4	5	Hire or Employ Later

Total Number of Points: _____

COMMENTS:_____
_____
_____

Interviewer Signature: _____ Date: _____

Resource H

Self-Evaluation Rubrics for
Basic Teacher Computer Use

Please judge your level of achievement in each of the following competencies. Circle the number which best reflects your current level of skill attainment. (Be honest, but be kind.) At the end of the training program, you will complete the same set of rubrics that will reflect your level of skill attainment at that time. (Level 3 is considered mastery.) This tool is to help measure the effectiveness of our training program, and to help you do a self-analysis to determine the areas in which you should continue to learn and practice. Keep a copy of these rubrics to refer to during the training.

I. Basic computer operation
    Level 1 I do not use a computer.
    Level 2 I can use the computer to run a few specific, preloaded programs. It has little effect on either my work or home life. I am somewhat anxious I might damage the machine or its programs.
    Level 3 I can set up my computer and peripheral devices, load software, print, and use most of the operating system tools like the scrapbook, clock, note pad, Find command, and trash can (recycling bin). I can format a data disk.
    Level 4 I can run two programs simultaneously, and have several windows open at the same time. I can customize the look and sounds of my computer. I use techniques like shift-clicking to work with multiple files. I look for programs and techniques to maximize my operating system. I feel confident enough to teach others some basic operations.

II. File management
    Level 1 I do not save any documents I create using the computer.
    Level 2 I save documents I've created but I cannot choose where they are saved. I do not back up my files.
    Level 3 I have a filing system for organizing my files, and can locate files quickly and reliably. I back up my files to floppy disk or other storage device on a regular basis.
    Level 4 I regularly run a disk-optimizer on my hard drive, and use a backup program to make copies of my files on a weekly basis. I have a system for archiving files that I do not need on a regular basis to conserve my computer's hard drive space.

III. Word processing
    Level 1 I do not use a word processor, nor can I identify any uses or features it might have that would benefit the way I work.

Level 2 I occasionally use the word processor for simple documents that I know I will modify and use again. I generally find it easier to hand write or type most written work I do.

Level 3 I use the word processor for nearly all my written professional work: memos, tests, worksheets, and home communication. I can edit, spell check, and change the format of a document. I can paginate, preview, and print my work. I feel my work looks professional.

Level 4 I use the word processor not only for my work, but have used it with students to help them improve their communication skills.

IV. Spreadsheet use

Level 1 I do not use a spreadsheet, nor can I identify any uses or features it might have that would benefit the way I work.

Level 2 I understand the use of a spreadsheet and can navigate within one. I can create a simple spreadsheet that adds a column of numbers.

Level 3 I use a spreadsheet for several applications. These spreadsheets use labels, formulas, and cell references. I can change the format of the spreadsheet by changing column widths and text style. I can use the spreadsheet to make a simple graph or chart.

Level 4 I use the spreadsheet not only for my work, but have used it with students to help them improve their own data keeping and analysis skills.

V. Database use

Level 1 I do not use a database, nor can I identify any uses or features it might have that would benefit the way I work.

Level 2 I understand the use of a database and can locate information within one that has been pre-made. I can add or delete data in a database.

Level 3 I use databases for personal applications. I can create an original database, defining fields and creating layouts. I can find, sort, and print information in layouts that are clear and useful to me.

Level 4 I can use formulas with my database to create summaries of numerical data. I can use database information to mail merge in a word processing document. I use the database not only for my work, but have used it with students to help them improve their own data keeping and analysis skills.

VI. Graphics use

Level 1 I do not use graphics in my word processing or presentations, nor can I identify any uses or features they might have that would benefit the way I work.

Level 2 I can open and create simple pictures with the painting and drawing programs. I can use programs like PrintShop or SuperPrint.

Level 3 I use both pre-made clip art and simple original graphics in my word processed documents and presentations. I can edit clip art, change its size, and place it on a page. I can purposefully use most of the drawing tools, and can group and ungroup objects. I can use the clipboard to take graphics from one application for use in another. The use of graphics in my work helps clarify or amplify my message.

Level 4 I use graphics not only for my work, but have used it with students to help them improve their own communications. I can use graphics and the word processor to create a professional-looking newsletter.

VII. Hypermedia use

Level 1 I do not use hypermedia (HyperStudio), nor can I identify any uses or features it might have that would benefit the way I work.

Level 2 I can navigate through a pre-made hypermedia program.

Level 3 I can create my own hypermedia stacks for information presentation. These stacks use navigation buttons, sounds, dissolves, graphics, and text fields. I can use an LCD projection device to display the presentation to a class.

Level 4 I use hypermedia with students who are making their own stacks for information storage and presentation.

VIII. Network use

Level 1 I do not use the online resources available in my building, nor can I identify any uses or features they might have that would benefit the way I work.

Level 2 I understand that there is a large amount of information available to teachers that can be accessed through networks, including the Internet. With the help of the media specialist, I can use the resources on the network in our building.

Level 3 I use the networks to access professional and personal information from a variety of sources including networked CD-ROM reference materials, online library catalogs, the ERIC database, and the World Wide Web. I have an e-mail account that I use on a regular basis.

Level 4 Using telecommunications, I am an active participant in online discussions and can download files and programs from remote computers. I use telecommunications with my students.

IX. Student assessment

Level 1 I do not use the computer for student assessment.

Level 2 I understand that there are ways I can keep track of student progress using the computer. I keep some student-produced materials on the computer, and write evaluations of student work and notes to parents with the word processor.

Level 3 I effectively use an electronic grade book to keep track of student data and/or I keep portfolios of student-produced materials on the computer. I use the electronic data during parent/teacher conferences.

Level 4 I rely on the computer to keep track of outcomes and objectives individual students have mastered. I use that information to determine assignments, teaching strategies, and groupings.

X. Ethical use understanding

Level 1 I am not aware of any ethical issues surrounding computer use.

Level 2 I know that some copyright restrictions apply to computer software.

Level 3 I clearly understand the difference between freeware, shareware, and commercial software, and the fees involved in the use of each. I know the programs for which the district or my building holds a site license. I understand the school board policy on the use of copyrighted materials. I demonstrate ethical usage of all software and let my students know my personal stand on legal and moral issues involving technology. I know and enforce the school's technology policies and guidelines, including its Internet Acceptable Use Policy. I have a personal philosophy I can articulate regarding the use of technology in education.

Level 4 I am aware of other controversial aspects of technology use including data privacy, equitable access, and free speech issues. I can speak to a variety of technology issues at my professional association meetings, to parent groups, and to the general community.

SOURCE: U.S. Department of Education (1998).

Resource I

Rubric for Assessing Electronic Portfolios

Skill	*1*	*2*	*3*	*4*	*5*
Mechanics	Most links do not work, many dead ends, numerous spelling errors	5-10 links don't work, many dead ends, links not clear, all linear, numerous spelling errors	3-4 links don't work, some links go to dead ends, numerous spelling errors	Most links work, links are clearly labeled, easy to navigate stack, few spelling errors	Multi-linked pages, all links work, links clearly labeled, no spelling errors
Structure	One stack or each card saved as a stack, named incorrectly	One stack or each card saved as a stack, some named correctly	One stack, named correctly, no table of contents	4-6 stacks, named correctly, table of contents	Multi-stacks, named, .stk table of contents, easy navigation
Graphics	No graphics	Only clip art, no scanned pictures, little use of drawing tools	Clip art, scanned pictures not clear, little use of drawing tools	Clip art, clear scanned pictures, some use of drawing tools	Clip art, clear scanned pictures, varied use of drawing tools
Use of Tools	No special tools used	Built-in sound used but irrelevant to card	Good use of sound and one special effect	Original relevant sound and at least one New Button Action (NBA)	Original relevant sound, video, animation, and at least one NBA
Content Relevancy[a]	Only personal information	Mostly personal information, no coursework or resume	Few examples of coursework, field experience, hobbies and interests, no resume	Examples of coursework, lessons, related field experience, hobbies and interests and resume	Good examples of coursework, lessons, related field experience, hobbies and interests and resume
Captions/ Reflections	No captions or reflective pieces	Few captions, mostly descriptive, not telling why pieces were included	Adequate captions but descriptive only	Good use of captions but greater depth of reflection needed	Excellent captions provide links between experiences and learning theory, thoughtful reflections explain why pieces included

SOURCE: Morris (2003).

NOTES: a. This may vary depending on the kind of portfolio that you are constructing.

Resource J
Online Resources for Electronic Portfolios

- Adobe PhotoShop & Acrobat. Includes many other multimedia tools: www.adobe.com/main.html
- Apple Quick Time: www.apple.com/quicktime/products/
- Apple iMovie: www.apple.com/imovie/
- Appleworks: www.apple.com/appleworks/
- Astound: www.astound.com/wc/index2.html
- ClarisWorks & Filemaker Pro: Claris Corporation 800-325-2747
- David Niguidula and Hilarie Davis Web site on digital portfolios: home.att.net/~digitalportfolio/
- Designer Software—Electronic Portfolio Toolkit: 847-516-8210
- Digital Chisel by Pierian Springs Software: 800-472-8578, www.epinions.com/Reference_Education-Other-Pierian_Spring_Software
- Electronic Portfolio: Scholastic Inc. 800-541-5513, www.scholastic.com/home.htm
- Electronic Portfolio by Learning Quest: www.learnng-quest.com/ephome.html
- Feasible Electronic Student Portfolios: Global Networking for the Self-Directed Learner in the Digital Age: www.mehs.educ.state.ak.us/portfolios/why_digitalportfolios.html
- Filemaker Pro from Filemaker, Inc.: www.filemaker.com/education/educators.html
- Grady Profile Portfolio Assessment from Aurbach and Associates: 800-77GRADY, www.aurbach.com/gp2.html
- Helen Barrett's Electronic Portfolios: www.electronicportfolios.com
- Hyperstudio: 800-HYPERSTUDIO, www.hyperstudio.com
- IBM's School Vista Assessment Suite by IBM Corporation: www.solutions.ibm.com/k12/solutions/tools/svassess.html
- Macromedia Authorware: www.macromedia.com/software/authorware/
- Macromedia Dreamweaver: www.macromedia.com/software/ dreamweaver/
- Macromedia Director: www/macromedia.com/software/director/
- Martin Kimeldorf's Portfolio Library: www.amby.com/kimeldorf/portfolio/
- Microsoft Web authoring tools (FrontPage) and multimedia: www.microsoft.com/homepage/ms.htm
- Microsoft PowerPoint: www.microsoft.com/office/powerpoint/default.asp
- Netscape Composer: wp.netscape.com/communicator/composer/v4.0/index.html
- Portfolios and Self-Assessment—Houghton-Mifflin's Education Place: www.hmco.com/hmco/school/rdg/res/literacy/assess7.html
- Roger Wagner's page on Creating Electronic Portfolios with HyperStudio: www.hyperstudio.com/resource/profdev/portfolio.html
- School Odyssey: www.ideasconsulting.com

- Sunburst Portfolio Builder: 800-321-7511, www.sunburst-store.com
- Superlink from Alchemedia, Inc.: www.alchemediainc.com/slfeatr.html
- Technology Applications for a Learning Network: www.applications. edreform.net
- Toolbook Content Authoring Products from Click2learn, Inc.: 800-448-6543, www.asymetrix.com/en/toolbook/index.asp
- Yahoo Listserv Electronic Portfolios: eportfolios-subscribe@yahoogroups.com

References

Adorno, T. W. (1989). *Kierkegaard: Construction of the aesthetic* (R. Hullot-Kentor, Trans.). Minneapolis: University of Minnesota Press. (Original work published 1933)

Albion College Department of Education. (2003). *What is a digital portfolio?* Retrieved November 8, 2002, from www.albion.edu/education/portfolio. asp

Ash, G. E. (2003). *Creating and using portfolios on the alphabet superhighway.* Retrieved October 30, 2002, from www.ash.udel.edu/ash/teacher/portfolio. html

Barrett, H. C. (1998). *What to consider when planning for electronic portfolios.* Retrieved October 29, 2002, from www.electronicportfolios.com/portfolios/ LLTOct98.html

Barrett, H. C. (2000). *Create your own electronic portfolio.* Retrieved November 18, 2002, from www.electronicportfolios.com/portfolios/iste2k.html

Barton, J., & Collins, A. (Eds.). (1997). *Portfolio assessment: A handbook for educators.* Menlo Park, CA: Addison-Wesley.

Bergman, T. (2003). *Digital portfolios.* Retrieved October 29, 2002, from www. mehs.educ.state.ak.us/portfolios/portfolio.html

Boody, R., & Montecinos, C. (1997, September). Hiring a new teacher? Ask for a portfolio. *Principal,* 34-35.

Borden, V., & Thomas, T. (2001, June 26). *A baker's dozen lessons learned about what it takes to develop and sustain electronic portfolios for program and institutional assessment.* Paper presented at the AAHE Assessment Conference, Denver, Colorado. Retrieved November 4, 2002, from www.imir.iupui.edu/portfolio/lessons.htm

Boulware, Z. (1998, September). *Using CD-ROM technology with preservice teachers to develop portfolios. The Journal,* Article 2053. Retrieved November 4, 2002, from www.thejournal.com/magazine/vault/ A2053B.cfm

Boulware, Z., Bratina, T., Holt, D., & Johnson, A. C. (1997, April). *Developing professional portfolios using CD-ROM technology as a teaching-learning tool.* Paper presented at the 8th International Conference of the Society for Information Technology and Teacher Education, Orlando, Florida.

Bunting, C. (1997). Fostering teacher growth from within. *Principal, 77,* 35.

Campbell, D., Cignetti, P., Melenyzer, B., Nettles, D., & Wyman, R. (1997). *How to develop a professional portfolio: A manual for teachers.* Boston: Allyn & Bacon.

Career Development Center. (1998). *Questions to ask in education interviews.* Retrieved October 7, 1998, from www.snybuf.edu/cdc/resume/eduques.htm

College of William & Mary, Office of Career Services. (1996). *Interview questions (teaching).* Retrieved October 3, 1998, from staff.wm.edu/career/02/Student/Interview/InterviewIndex.cfm

Dietz, M. (1995). Using portfolios as a framework for professional development. *Journal of Staff Development, 16,* 40-43.

Doolittle, P. (1994, April). *Teacher portfolio assessment.* Washington, DC: ERIC Clearinghouse on Assessment and Evaluation. (ERIC Document Reproduction Service No. ED385608).

Evans, M. (1997). *Student portfolio for competency seminar.* Unpublished manuscript, East Central University, Ada, OK.

Family Educational Rights and Privacy Act, 20 U.S.C. § 1232g; 34 CFR § 99 (1974).

Frank, W. S. (1998). *200 cover letters for job hunters: Twenty-eight common mistakes.* Retrieved October 1, 1998, from www.careerlab.com.

Gardner, H. (1993). *Creating minds: An anatomy of creativity seen through the lives of Freud, Einstein, Picasso, Stravinsky, Eliot, Graham and Gandhi.* New York: Basic Books.

Geltner, B. (1993, October). *Integrating formative portfolio assessment, reflective practice and cognitive coaching into preservice preparation.* Paper presented at the annual meeting of the University Council for Educational Administration, Houston, TX.

Gilreath, C. (1997, Fall). *Partial requirement for instructional competency I.* Unpublished manuscript, East Central University, Ada, OK.

Goleman, D., Kaufman, P., & Ray, M. (1992). *The creative spirit.* New York: Dutton.

Habermas, J. (1985). Hermeneutics and the social sciences. In K. Vollmer (Ed.), *The hermeneutic reader* (pp. 293-320). New York: Continuum.

Holton, K. (1997, Spring). *Exit portfolio requirement for professional clinical IV.* Unpublished manuscript, East Central University, Ada, OK.

Hutchins, J. (1997, Fall). *Partial portfolio requirement for instructional competency seminar.* Unpublished manuscript, East Central University, Ada, OK.

International Society for Technology in Education (ISTE). (n.d.). *Standards and performance indicators for all teachers.* Retrieved November 18, 2002, from cnets.iste.org/teachers/t_stands.html

International Society for Technology in Education (ISTE). (2003). *National Educational Technology Standards.* Retrieved November 18, 2002, from cnets.iste.org/index.shtml

Interstate New Teacher Assessment and Support Consortium (INTASC). (1998). *Model standards for beginning teacher licensing and development.* Retrieved October 3, 1998, from www.ccsso.org/Projects/

Interview Experts. (1998). *Interviewing questions*. Retrieved May 17, 1998, from www.interviewexperts.com

Jacobson, L. (1997, March). Portfolios playing increasing role in teacher hiring. *Education Week*. Retrieved April 15, 1998, from www.edweek.org

Kalamazoo College. (1998). *Starting a self-presentation portfolio*. Retrieved March 7, 1998, from http://www.kzoo.edu/pfolio

Kennedy, J. L. (1995, August 13). Job Talk. *Tribune Media Services*. Retrieved October 2, 2002, from www.amby.com/kimeldorf/portfolio/p_mk-02.html

McLaughlin, M., & Vogt, M. E. (1996). *Portfolios in teacher education*. Newark, DE: International Reading Association.

Michalski, R. S. (1987). Learning strategies and automated knowledge acquisition: An overview. In B. Leonard (Ed.), *Computational models of learning* (pp. 1-21). New York: Springer-Verlag.

Morris, J. L. (2003). *Rubric for assessing electronic portfolios*. University of Vermont, Department of Education. Retrieved November 18, 2002, from www.uvm.edu/~jmorris/rubricep.html

Morris, V. C. (1969). *Existentialism in education: What it means*. New York: Harper & Row.

Moustakas, C. E. (1981). Heuristic research. In P. Reason & J. Rowan (Eds.), *Human Inquiry*. New York: John Wiley.

Murray, D. (1968). *A writer teaches writing: A practical method of teaching composition*. New York: Holt, Rinehart & Winston.

National Board for Professional Teaching Standards (NBPTS). (1998). *The portfolio*. Retrieved November 6, 2002, from www.nbpts.org/candidates/portfolios. cfm

National Council for Accreditation of Teacher Education (NCATE). (1997). *Technology and the new professional teacher: Preparing for the 21st century classroom*. Retrieved November 18, 2002, from ncate.org/accred/projects/tech/tech-21.htm

National Council for Accreditation of Teacher Education (NCATE). (2003). *Frequently asked questions*. Retrieved November 18, 2002, from ncate.org/standard/ faq_standards.htm

Niguidula, D. (1993, October). *The digital portfolio: A richer picture of student performance*. Coalition of Essential Schools. Retrieved October 29, 2002, from mel.lib.mi.us/education/edu-assess.html

Oklahoma State Board of Education. (1996). *Oklahoma general competencies for teacher licensure and certification*. Oklahoma City, OK: Author.

Robelen, E. (1999). *The promise and the pitfalls*. Association for Supervision and Curriculum Development INFOBRIEF. Retrieved November 4, 2002, from www.ascd.org/readingroom/infobrief/9903.html

Sanders, T. (1997, Spring). *Exit portfolio requirement for professional clinical teaching IV*. Unpublished manuscript, East Central University, Ada, OK.

Sewell, M., Marczak, M., & Horn, M. (1997). *The use of portfolio assessment in evaluation*. San Diego, CA: County Office of Education.

Tuttle, H. G. (1997). *The multimedia report: Electronic portfolios tell a personal story*. Retrieved October 30, 2002, from www.infotoday.com/ MMSchools/jan97mms/portfol.htm

University of Colorado. (1998). *School district interview questions for teachers.* Retrieved 1998, from www.cudenver.edu/public/career/tchint97.html

University of Nebraska. (1998). *The structured interview.* Retrieved August 11, 2003, from www.unl.edu/careers/prepare/questionsbyemployer.htm

University of Northern Iowa, College of Education. (1998). *A guide to the development of a professional portfolio.* Retrieved August 12, 2003, from ci.coe.uni.edu/portfolio/

U.S. Department of Education. (1993). *Using technology to support education reform.* Washington, DC: Government Printing Office.

U.S. Department of Education. (1998). *An educator's guide to evaluating the use of technology in schools and classrooms.* Washington, DC: Government Printing Office.

Wiedmer, T. L. (1998). Digital portfolios: Capturing and demonstrating skills and levels of performance. *Phi Delta Kappan, 79,* 586-589.

Index

CORWIN PRESS

The Corwin Press logo—a raven striding across an open book—represents the union of courage and learning. Corwin Press is committed to improving education for all learners by publishing books and other professional development resources for those serving the field of K–12 education. By providing practical, hands-on materials, Corwin Press continues to carry out the promise of its motto: "**Helping Educators Do Their Work Better.**"